James and Jennie's honest, ⟨ experiences will be a great ⟨ suffering, and to friends and It is full of godly wisdom and

Vaughan Roberts

Rector of St Ebbe's, Oxford and Director of Proclamation Trust

This book challenges us to be 'strong and courageous' when supporting the suffering. I saw immediate fruit from the Muldoon's teaching to be more intentional, to acknowledge and so validate the struggles of others, and to unapologetically give them Christ! A must-read!

Natalie Brand

Author and tutor for women, Union School of Theology, Wales

In *Helping the Suffering*, James and Jennie share their poignant and personal story of suffering. It's a hard story, but not a hopeless story. And out of the ashes of their sorrow emerges helpful insight and practical takeaways for those who walk alongside others in their sufferings. In *Helping the Suffering*, God's faithfulness shines forth on every page.

Christina Fox

Writer, speaker, and author of several books including
Closer than a Sister

Many people don't know how to walk well with those who are suffering, because they don't really know what it feels like from the inside, or because they're too afraid of 'getting it wrong' to take the first step. This refreshingly honest book shines a light into some dark places, and gives practical advice on what has been helpful (and what has not). It is also an encouraging story of authentic faith in times of trial, and a God whose ways may sometimes seem strange, but whose love really does endure forever. I'm confident this book will help God's people 'weep with those who weep' and shine forth the comfort and mercy of Christ Jesus.

Matt Searles
Director of Training, South Central Gospel Partnership
Author of *Tumbling Sky: Psalms for Weary Souls*

Suffering is not a competition, but if it were, Jennie and James would be well ahead of most of us. But out of their experience of what they describe as 'the unpredictable course of grief', comes this honest and practical handbook. For those of us who guiltily hang back around suffering friends, this book is a nudge in the ribs. 'Go on. You can help and here is how.'

Ann Benton
Author and family conference speaker, Guildford, England

What a helpful and inspiring book! In just two hours of reading, Jennie and James let you in on the painful road they have had to travel. They encourage you to see the faithfulness of God and to be a better friend to those who are suffering.

Will Stileman
Vicar, St Mary's, Maidenhead, UK

In an easy style, and with honesty and tears, James and Jennie tell us their story of suffering. We learn that the Lord leads us through situations which are too much for us to bear, but are not too much for Him to carry us through. With an open Bible, and with a wisdom born of their own experience, they then move on to give us a host of practical suggestions about helping the suffering. It is all challenging and wonderful.

Stuart Olyott

Retired pastor, author and missionary

I am glad I have read this book and have no qualms in highly recommending it.

It begins by outlining several years of the authors' family life, years in which they were challenged by disability, cancer, other serious illnesses and the loss of several of those who were nearest and dearest to them. Being a ministry family did not give them immunity to life's troubles. Instead, they had to bear them in the public eye, which is the lot of ministry families.

In the second half of the book we discover what helped them through their hard years and what garrisons them whatever their future holds. Their help was found in Bible, in their own devotions and the prayer support of others and through the truths of God's Word applied to their situation. Friends, especially those who were prepared to hang on in over the long term, were a great help as was the assurance that God makes no mistakes in His providential dealings with His children.

The book ends with a ringing affirmation that Jesus remembers and understands. Jesus remembers the cross and what the worst of life's troubles feels like. 'That is compassion written in the largest letters upon the canvas of the universe.'

Irene Howat
Author of numerous books, including *Pain, My Companion*

Suffering is folded into the fabric of our lives. The only condition for suffering is to live long enough. In this moving book James and Jennie Muldoon share their story and draw out seven lessons which they have learned while in the furnace of affliction. The book is pastorally sensitive and biblically faithful. When we suffer we need truth, compassion and hope. This book will help you to find these things in Jesus.

Paul Mallard
Author of *Invest Your Suffering*
Pastor, Widcombe Baptist Church, Bath, UK

HELPING
the
SUFFERING

*Autobiographical insights
on supporting those in pain*

James & Jennie Muldoon

Copyright © James and Jennie Muldoon 2020

paperback ISBN 978-1-5271-0558-4
epub ISBN 978-1-5271-0620-8
mobi ISBN 978-1-5271-0621-5

Published in 2020
by
Christian Focus Publications Ltd,
Geanies House, Fearn, Ross-shire
IV20 1TW, Scotland
www.christianfocus.com

Cover design by Tiger Finch Creatives

Printed and bound by
Bell & Bain, Glasgow

CONTENTS

For Elly, Livia and Nate. Christ is risen!

Part I – Introduction

We've thought for some time about writing this book. About a decade ago, we entered into a time of suffering which was unlike anything we'd been through before. We'd suffered before that, for sure. Between us we'd experienced poverty and depression and loneliness and chronic health conditions, but 2010 heralded the start of a period when one experience of suffering seemed to domino over the top of another. We've had our lives and our service for the Lord Jesus Christ radically remodelled because of it. In particular we've learned, by God's grace, to support others in their times of suffering with more empathy and sensitivity. We've decided to write this book in the hope that we can help you to do the same.

We've set the book out in two parts.

Part One simply tells our story. We've tried to be open about what we experienced, about how we felt and about how the Lord and others supported us in our trials. We've wanted to do this for two reasons. First, we're very thankful to the Lord for sustaining us through those times and through ongoing difficulties since then. Second, we realize that our sufferings are not the same as other people's sufferings. There's a sense in which each individual type of suffering brings with it its own particular suite of pangs. We wanted to give you some context by being clear about our experiences.

As you read our story you may feel that our lives are just rammed full of misery. Frankly, as we've read back what we've written, sometimes it does look as though a black dog has sat with us as we've put our experiences into writing. In fact our lives are filled with joy. There have been extreme joys in the tough times, and there have been the normal joys of life in the times where we haven't really been up against it. We wouldn't want you to get the impression that we're glum, despondent, downbeat types. We relish life and – though sometimes we say this through gritted teeth – we wouldn't want to have any other life than the one which the Lord has chosen for us. Please read what we're writing in that context!

Part Two is made up of lessons we've learned, as we've gone through our various situations, about supporting others in suffering. We'll have a separate introduction to that part when we get there.

We're grateful for the support of many as we've been writing down our thoughts and experiences. We're thankful for our church family giving James a sabbatical period to create the space needed to be able to write. We're thankful to a small group of people at the church who have been our sabbatical support group and who have helped us along the way. We're thankful to our family and friends who have encouraged us over the years. And we're especially thankful to the Lord Jesus Christ who is stunningly faithful and compassionate.

1

Us

Most of us have known the experience of moving to a new place and of having to introduce ourselves to a new set of acquaintances. It can be easy to rerun the same conversation time and time again.

'Hello, I'm Ryan.'

'Hello, Ryan. I'm Bob. Where are you from?'

'I'm from Stevenage.'

'Oh. And what do you do?'

'I'm the person who puts that jelly into pork pies.'

So here are our introductions, just so that you don't have to ask.

James was born in the East Midlands of England in the early 1970s. Before his second birthday his parents moved to a village in the East Anglian Fens. His father had been converted in his teens but had drifted from the Lord soon after that. When James was six, his dad suddenly came back to the Lord and, by God's grace, his mother was converted soon afterwards. As a family, they began to attend a church which had been Strict and Particular, but which had become Particular and Not-So-Strict. James's sister, Morag, and brother, Samuel, were both born in the Fens.

James doesn't know when he was converted, but it was certainly before he was ten that he'd repented of his sin and put his faith in the Lord Jesus Christ. At primary school, he was an outrageous, in-your-face, kind of evangelist – or to put it another way, a bit of a pain in the neck. At secondary school, however, he was cowed into silence about his faith. He'd speak up for the Lord if it were absolutely necessary, but if not, he'd keep his mouth shut. He was a wishy-washy Christian.

James attended school and found that he was quite good at subjects like Latin which were practically useless. He was offered a place at university to study Classics on the basis that he took a gap year, which he accepted. That meant having a year out which he hadn't planned to take, a year which turned out to be a big part of God's plan for his life.

As James was finishing school, a magazine from the London City Mission arrived, advertising the mission's one year scheme for 18- to 30-year-olds, then called Voluntary Evangelism. James applied, got a place, and moved to London. Within 48 hours of arriving, the Lord had dealt with him and had given him a passion for Jesus which he hadn't had before. From then on he knew that he was going to be in full-time Christian ministry of some sort eventually. At the mission, he started preaching, did lots of youth work, did lots of door-to-door evangelism, and grew up.

Following this, James completed three years away at university, after which he moved back home to his parents' place. After all, you don't expect a job with a Classics degree, do you? He found work as a pallbearer ('a job for life'), worked for a church in Croatia for a few months during the war between the former Yugoslav republics, and finally settled down in a more permanent role working for a pensions company. We'll leave his story there for a while.

Jennie was born in Surrey in the later 1970s to a British father and an Australian mother who had met on the mission field in Bolivia. Jennie is the youngest of their four children. Her brother, Iain, and sister, Pamela, were born in South America; she and her brother Andrew were born in the UK.

From Surrey, Jennie moved to Leicestershire and then Lincolnshire, her father now a church minister. Her childhood was full of church and church-related events. She loved being with people at church. She loved the church youth groups and camps. She loved visiting people in their homes with her father. She loved older members of the different congregations who showed practical love and who prayed. She was always hearing the gospel message, and her parents always had it as a priority in their lives. But she longed not only to know the gospel message but to feel it and to pray as though she really meant it.

Assurance was a continual problem for Jennie while she was growing up. She can remember many times when she prayed, 'Lord forgive me; I want to be a Christian!' But then the next day she didn't feel any different and life would carry on as normal.

As time progressed Jennie began to realize that she was looking for a bright light Damascus Road experience. She realized there probably wouldn't be any radical change in her outward behaviour because she had actually been quite good anyway!

One summer Jennie was due to go away on a church camp. She became so fearful of going on yet another camp without being sure whether she was a Christian that she knew she had to do something about it. So after a very late-night discussion with her mother, they prayed together. She knew, following that prayer, that whether she had been a Christian before or not, she certainly was one now. She had once again asked Jesus to forgive her sin, had said sorry for this and had devoted her life to live for Jesus – but somehow this time she knew that this was it and that she didn't need to keep on asking.

Life carried on. In her early teens, Jennie moved from Leicestershire to the Fens, leaving friends and a familiar routine behind. This was hard but a new school, church and routines soon settled life down. A year after the move to the Fens she was baptized in her local church. Friends at school knew she was a Christian and would occasionally come along with her to church events. She became quite outspoken in RE classes with her devout Jewish teacher. He kept fighting his corner but did come along to a baptism – as long as Jennie promised to go along to a Jewish ceremony!

There was a youth group at the church and the group would meet regularly with other like-minded churches in the area. This was a great encouragement and many lifelong friendships were formed at that time.

Jennie finished school and worked for three years in the same pensions company as James. In her job she had to deal with lots of stressed and complaining people, a good training ground in arguing and standing fast!

We met on 9 April 1993. Jennie's dad was about to become the new pastor of the church James already belonged to. After Jennie and her family had been at the church for two years, James was starting to feel rather keen on her, but it was a slow-burning relationship. Jennie took some time to be wooed by James's 'interesting' sense of humour. We attended various groups at the church together, we had trips to Sizewell B nuclear power station together and we gradually fell in love.

Having grown up as a pastor's daughter, Jennie was quite determined not to marry someone interested in ministry and especially someone thinking of becoming a pastor. The Lord had other ideas. So on 25 July 1998, three years later, we were married, planning within the next year or two to go off to Bible College to prepare for full-time Christian ministry. We had a little house where we painted the walls colours which we would never dream of using today.

Just over two years later, in September 2000, we moved to South Wales to go to theological college, where we both studied for three excellent years. Following that, James became an Assistant Pastor in the same town while Jennie started training to be an Occupational Therapist. After six years in South Wales we moved to Berkshire in 2006 where James became a Co-Pastor, and, at the time of writing, that's where we still are.

2

Infertility

We knew before we got married that we were going to struggle with infertility. It wasn't something which worried us in the early days of our marriage; in fact, we told people back then that we weren't too concerned whether we had children or not – there just seemed to be many years in front of us to think about that. Nevertheless, it was always in the back of Jennie's mind and as the years went by, it started to cast a longer and longer shadow over our lives.

According to the UK's National Health Service (see www.nhs.uk/conditions/infertility – accessed 13 September 2018), infertility is when a couple fails to conceive despite having regular unprotected sexual intercourse. In our day, a diagnosis of infertility was generally given after this had gone on for two years of trying, though the best advice was to seek medical help if nothing happened after one year of trying.

When infertility strikes, it can hurt. Think of Hannah's experience in I Samuel 1:10-11. She's been unable to conceive. And here's what it does to her.

> Deeply hurt, Hannah prayed to the Lord and wept with many tears. Making a vow, she pleaded, 'Lord of Armies, if you will take notice of your servant's affliction, remember and not forget me, and give your servant a son, I will give him to the Lord all the days of his life, and his hair will never be cut.'

There is highly emotive language there. Hannah experiences bitterness of soul. She weeps with many tears. She talks about her affliction, her misery. She longs for a son, and she is ready to dedicate him to the Lord for life – if only he comes.

And that's what infertility can feel like. It's heartache. It's like bereavement, grief over a person who never was. It's an aching within. It's despair, hopelessness, abandonment. It brings fears of loneliness in old age. It makes you wonder whether God really loves you. It makes you feel inadequate, like there's something wrong with you.

By 2008, when we'd been married for ten years, we knew that it was the right time for us to confront our infertility medically. We prayed. We shared with close family, a few friends, and the elders of our church. And we started to make medical appointments.

One of the curious things about infertility is that the husband and the wife can feel quite differently about it. A couple of years later, in 2010, we were asked to contribute to an excellent book about infertility called *Just the Two of Us?* by Eleanor Margesson and Sue McGowan.

Here is part of what Jennie wrote.

'Infertility for me is a very difficult, exhausting and challenging road to travel. I sometimes feel very alone. My husband is very supportive and seeks to understand where he does not have the feelings that I might. Few people … understand or even remember that this is such a problem for us. Even if people remember, they forget to ask or are too embarrassed to do so. Most of the time I am screaming inwardly for people to ask me how I am, to give me a cuddle, or simply to listen and not say anything.' She was acknowledging there that, though James also felt our infertility deeply he didn't always have the same strength of feeling about it. So, for his part, James wrote: 'When I see a young woman with a pushchair, I wish it was my wife. When I sense my wife's heart sinking because she sees the pride on a new mother's face, I grieve with her.' But there could be times when the ache was not as keen as Jennie's.

As a result of our slightly different perspectives, it became vitally important that we saw the situation not as Jennie's problem nor as James's problem but as our problem. So we sought to share with each other, to pray with each other, to laugh with each other and to mourn with each other as much as we could.

Ironically, church can be a very hard place for those struggling with infertility. It can be really hard when there's news of another pregnancy. Or when couples who've only just got married conceive almost immediately. Or when families which are really large announce that another is on its way. Or when parents get stressed with their children for misbehaving and say, 'You must be glad you don't have kids when they behave like this!' Church can be a place of dread for those suffering from infertility.

And so it was that we were plunged into a merry-go-round of infertility treatments. We found the hospital treatment very clinical and sometimes felt like a specimen. The treatment was intrusive and emotionally draining. There were prods and pokes, cameras, scans, blood tests, questions and more questions, lectures on anatomy, lectures on diet and weight, questions about regularity of sex, and on and on it went. There were expectations, discouragements and confusion.

At times, the only thing which gave us any encouragement was the fact that we have a God who can ordain whatever He wills. Jennie wrote, 'I generally feel pessimistic about whether we will ever have children but know that I have to remember that God is in control. It is very difficult to remember this continually, and it is sometimes the last thing I want to hear said by someone else, but I know that this is the only thing that will keep me going and strengthen my faith.'

And then it happened! Our local hospital suggested some new medication which involved daily injections for a fortnight. A few weeks later, on 7 April, we discovered, to our absolute shock, that Jennie was expecting. We were on our way to visit friends in the north of England at the time. We were staying in an appalling hotel in the Midlands. The contrast between the new life which was just starting to grow inside Jennie and the grim surroundings was very striking. But we were able to thank God for answering the prayers of many years. We were equally overjoyed that another couple who'd been struggling with infertility along with us conceived at almost exactly the same time. God had been good to us.

And so the scans began. We had a seven-week scan which showed a little heartbeat. We had the usual twelve-week scan which showed our baby at about two inches long. And we waited for our twenty-week scan which was to happen on 23 July.

3

20 Weeks

It's a Friday afternoon. It's 23 July 2010. And it's time for our 20-week scan. Along we go with no concerns.

The scan began early in the afternoon and it all started off just like all the other scans we'd had up to that point. And then, suddenly, the sonographer said, 'We've got a problem here.' We both thought that she meant that our baby wouldn't get into the right position to be scanned or that there was some problem with her equipment. But her next sentence changed our lives radically. 'I think your baby's got spina bifida.'

It was all so matter-of-fact. Jennie burst into tears immediately and James moved over to hold her. The sonographer realized how it must have come across and switched into sympathetic mode. Nevertheless, she didn't want to be pressed on the details; only a doctor could confirm the diagnosis.

Given that it was a Friday afternoon, there were no specialists working in the hospital at the time. We were given an appointment for the following Monday. It was to be one of the longest weekends we've ever spent.

The scan was almost over before we realized that we hadn't asked whether the baby was a boy or a girl. The sonographer said, 'Oh, you still want to know?' sounding astonished that we cared. When we then asked for some pictures, she again seemed surprised.

With hindsight, we're not too shocked at her reaction. We later found out that in about 80 per cent of the diagnoses of spina bifida given at the 20-week scan that year, the pregnancy was terminated. Our sonographer probably imagined that we'd be heading in the same direction.

She started scanning again and half-heartedly produced a couple of prints for us. She also told us that we were expecting a little girl. Hearing that, in a way which is hard for us to explain, was like a breath of fresh air in our gloom. Yes, we were facing uncertain times, maybe agonising times, but just to hear that we were expecting a girl was like a wave of normality in the midst of a sea of anxiety.

Straight after the initial scan, we drove to the edge of a park near the hospital. We sat there in the car stunned. We hugged each other. We wept together. We immediately clicked into worst-case-scenario mode, and a hundred different questions drove themselves into our minds. But alongside all of this, there was a strange sense of the presence of God with us. Right from the very moment we heard the news, we had a keen sense of the fact that God was in control and that He knew what He was doing, even if we didn't.

We remember some of the things which we said to each other then, though the whole afternoon passed in a strange blur. 'God can heal our little girl. But if He chooses not to, we have to trust Him to give us help for every crisis we face. He has given us a very special little girl and we are going to love her with everything we have and are.' We prayed through the tears and asked for God's help for whatever was ahead of us.

After we'd sat in our car on the edge of the park for an hour – we remember a couple in the car behind ours kissing and cuddling and carrying on without a care in the world – we drove home. We knew from the word 'go' that we wanted to enlist as much prayer support as we could, so we emailed the elders of our church, spread the situation out in front of them, and asked them to pray. We also emailed the church home groups to ask them to pray. We decided that we wanted to be with close family, so we travelled the 130 miles to see our parents, all of whom lived in the same village.

The journey was a horrible one. As we drove, we talked over thoughts like: 'Children are so cruel and they're going to give our little girl an awful time!' We were weeping as we drove along the road. We got stuck in traffic jams. We were hungry but didn't want to eat, though we knew we had to. We stopped at a McDonalds – for many years afterwards we avoided driving past that McDonalds because the memories of that journey and that day were too painful. Even today McDonalds still gives Jennie the creeps!

We'd already let both sets of parents know that there was a problem. Jennie's mother had been a midwife and she'd looked after a number of babies with spina bifida. When we arrived, there were instant hugs and tears. We were able just to be together and to support one another.

We have all kinds of tear-dampened memories of that weekend. Jennie remembers her side of the family all sitting round the kitchen table together talking. She remembers her Uncle Malcolm, visiting from Australia, feeling so sad that this had happened to her. She remembers her father buying her flowers, a gift of kindness which expressed how much he felt. James has memories of spending time with his side of the family. His brother, Sam, who we'll tell you more about later, asked if our baby was going to be in a wheelchair. We're thankful to God for the way as a wider family we were able to look after each other then.

Through all this time, the Lord gave us a strange sense of peace. We were very, very upset, yet we did not feel helpless. We knew that the Lord was in control. We knew that the Lord was our Father. We knew that He had His purposes in what we were starting to go through. We were given grace to trust Him and to lean upon Him. We are certain that the Lord was answering the prayers of many people who were already standing with us in prayer. The elders of our church had by now arranged a prayer meeting, for which we were so grateful, and we'd already started to receive messages of support from people all around the world.

Then we had to return home. James was due to lead the morning service at our home church and to preach at our evening service. We knew we would both be very upset, and we knew that facing lots of sympathetic people would be hard to deal with, so we put various measures in place.

We arranged for a good friend, the wife of one of the church elders, to sit with Jennie in a corner of the church. She reserved the back row seats for us and James arranged for an elder to lead in prayer in case he couldn't manage that.

Before we walked into the church building, two people had already hugged Jennie. This was too much for her, and she was in floods of tears. James circulated round the church and tried to talk with as many people as possible, partly so that Jennie wouldn't have to.

God gave us the grace to cope emotionally with the morning service. Some of the hymns were extremely moving. James was choking whilst standing in the pulpit singing hymns about God making us whole. Jennie left immediately after the service was over but James stayed and talked with people. By the evening service, both of us were feeling more solid, and we were able to cope and to chat with people afterwards.

Over the weekend Jennie carried out a little research about spina bifida. It was a condition which we'd heard of but which we didn't know too much about. She wanted to know something about it in advance of our appointment on the Monday. James, on the other hand, was content just to find out at the hospital.

And so the following morning we went back to the hospital. We were ushered in to see the specialist very quickly. She explained that she wouldn't be saying anything while she was carrying out the scan and that she would tell us all the details once she'd finished.

It was an unreal time. Jennie was realistic about the situation but still held on to some hope that our baby would not have spina bifida. Maybe the sonographer had got it wrong. Maybe the Lord had brought healing over the weekend. Maybe the condition would be one of the less severe forms of spina bifida. However, we wouldn't have been surprised if the situation was on the severe end of the spectrum either. Nevertheless, we felt a sense of assurance that God would work it all out. If it was best for Him to heal her, that was fine. If it was best for Him not to heal her, then that was fine and He would have to give us the strength to cope on a daily basis.

The scan didn't take too long. And then the doctor began to speak. She confirmed the diagnosis of spina bifida. She then went on to explain to us in great detail what that meant. Our baby girl's spine, she said, had not formed properly and her spinal cord was coming out into a pocket in her back (called a lesion). She explained that fluid was also collecting inside her head which was beginning to put pressure on her brain and might end up causing learning disabilities; this would become a condition called hydrocephalus. Our little girl would probably have to have an operation within a few days of being born to close up the pocket in her back. And she might also need an operation to drain the fluid from inside her skull by fitting a shunt.

All in all, the prognosis at this stage was grim. Our daughter would probably not be able to walk, and would have trouble with her bladder and bowels. Her life expectancy might be about ten years (something we now realize was based on some very out-of-date research). It was possible she might not even survive birth; an associated condition called a Chiari malformation might mean that she would be unable to breathe.

The doctor took her time. She offered us an abortion, which we declined. 'We're evangelical Christians,' we explained. 'Our little girl is very precious to us and we see her as a gift from God.' We're very grateful to the doctor that she didn't push the matter again after that.

Instead she went on to talk about the impact on us. There would be a financial impact, she said, because one of us would probably have to give up work to become a full-time carer. There would be a deep emotional impact. There could well be a negative impact upon our marriage. She asked about our support networks. Our heads were spinning with it all. In fact, afterwards we had to compare notes: James remembered some parts of what had been said, and Jennie remembered other parts. From then, we always made every effort to be present together at every appointment we had.

The whole appointment lasted more than an hour. Afterwards, we went back to the park where we'd been on Friday. Jennie phoned her parents. Her mum's heart was breaking over it all and Jennie remembers her shrill cry piercing her ears as she recounted to her what the doctors had said; in the end, her mum was so distressed she couldn't speak any longer. This was all the more poignant because Jennie's mum never cried. James rang his father, who broke down as he relayed the news to the rest of the family. We also called the other pastor of the church.

We again prayed and asked the Lord to take care of us and to help us to be the best parents we could possibly be for our little girl. We knew He could still heal her, but we were still very well aware that His plans might be different... and better.

We sent a number of emails to our church elders, to the church home groups, to friends, and to people from other churches. Once again, what we wanted above all else was to have as many people praying for us as quickly as possible. It was a real comfort for us to know that there were people from all over the world who were supporting us in prayer.

That was all in the morning. In the afternoon, we went back to the hospital. We met a paediatric doctor who took lots of time to explain everything again, which we found reassuring. We thank God for his gentle confidence in what he was saying. He was more optimistic about our daughter's likely lifespan.

That evening, we met with James's colleague and his wife. They pointed us to the word of God and read Psalm 139 with us. They said that, even though our little girl had spina bifida, she was still fearfully and wonderfully made. God was knitting her together in her mother's womb. All the days ordained for her were written in God's book. They were both visibly moved because of our situation, and we spent time praying together.

So ended one of the longest weekends of our lives, but, bizarrely, a weekend which drew us closer to each other, closer to others, and closer to God than we'd ever been before.

4

Rollercoaster

There's an old saying: 'Thousands can act, but few can wait.'
That's very true. We know that we are called to wait upon the
Lord, to wait for Him: passages like Lamentations 3:25-26 tell
us to do that. 'The Lord is good to those who wait for him, to the
person who seeks him. It is good to wait quietly for salvation
from the Lord.' We just find it confoundedly difficult to do so.
We'd rather do a million things than just wait.

From 23 July to 6 December 2010, the day our baby girl
was to be born, there was little we could do but wait upon
the Lord. At times we found the waiting unbearable, but, at the
same time, we found that the Lord gave us the patience we
needed.

It wasn't that we were doing nothing in that time. Jennie
continued to work as an Occupational Therapist at a local
hospice. James continued to serve as a pastor. And whatever

time that didn't involve, the NHS helpfully filled up for us with one appointment after another.

It was the scans which we found hardest to deal with. Not just one but two hospitals became involved in providing care for us; it was likely that Jennie was going to have to give birth in a specialist hospital an hour or so away from home. One fortnight, our local hospital wanted to scan Jennie; the next fortnight, the other hospital wanted to scan her. We ended up knowing far too much about our little girl's development.

For instance, one of the things the hospitals were most concerned about was the amount of fluid collecting inside our baby's head. They were worried about this because it would be an indication of whether hydrocephalus was developing and of how serious it was likely to be.

We had a scan at our local hospital in August, and things were encouraging. The amount of fluid hadn't increased too much, which was a very good sign. Other parts of her body were developing as expected. We went away praising God for answering our prayers.

Two weeks later we had a scan at the other hospital, and things were far from encouraging. The consultant felt that our baby's head was too small. As well as having spina bifida and hydrocephalus, he started to warn us that she might also have microcephaly and that she would probably die soon after birth. We went away devastated, reeling from yet another shock.

James remembers breaking down a couple of nights afterwards. He'd taken a couple of days off to paint our baby's room. It suddenly dawned on him in the middle of the night that he was decorating a room for someone who might not live to use it, yet at the same time he felt overwhelmed by a sense of God's goodness and control.

Two weeks after that we had a scan at our local hospital again. We told the doctor about the possibility of microcephaly. She did the usual measurements. And she concluded that there was nothing wrong with our baby's head size; it was small, but not too small. She looked at James and said, 'Well, you've got a small head!' She looked at Jennie and said, 'And you may have a small head too but I can't tell because you've got hair!' (Thankfully she then added something like, 'Not that having a small head means that your brain isn't up to much!')

It all felt like a rollercoaster. We'd have a good scan and go away elated. We'd have a bad scan, and we'd go away feeling as though we'd been kicked in the stomach.

And on and on it went. Waiting... Waiting on the Lord... Breaking under the anxiety and uncertainty... Knowing Him binding up our wounds...

As the weeks went by we continued to pray for her survival and her healing, but our prayers began to focus around two requests.

First, we prayed that our little girl would become a Christian. Praying for healing was important, but it was nowhere near as important as her coming to faith in the Lord Jesus Christ. Walking is great, but walking into a lost eternity makes walking seem relatively unimportant. We prayed and prayed for her to be saved.

Second, we prayed that we would see our little girl smile. It was a simple request. Our hearts longed for her to survive birth and (after a bit of development!) just to smile. It was something we could not take for granted, so we spread out our request before the Lord.

One of the things which kept us going was the support of other Christians. Our local church held numerous prayer meetings for us, and those meetings were impassioned and earnest. We were hearing regularly from Christians all over the world, some of whom said some extremely helpful things. Lots of people who'd had children with spina bifida and hydrocephalus contacted us. We were able to talk with some of them and to meet up with one family who happened to be in the hospital at the same time as us.

Throughout, we decided to tell people not just what was happening but also how we felt about it. Too many Christians feel they have to put on a brave face, to deny that hardships are hard. Some other Christians want to portray an idea that their lives are perfect and trouble-free, for whatever reason. We didn't want to do that. We felt shattered, torn, harassed and helpless. We wanted to be honest about that and at the same time we wanted to say how faithful the Lord was in all the turmoil.

At one point when we were sending an email update, we wrote this.

We still feel as though we're on a rollercoaster. Isaiah 41:10, a verse from last Sunday evening's sermon, has been very comforting to us. The Lord says, 'Do not fear, for I am with you; do not be afraid, for I am your God. I will strengthen you; I will help you; I will hold on to you with my righteous right hand.' We do fear from time to time. Before each scan, we get pretty anxious. But through all of that we know that we have someone with us who will strengthen us and help us and hold us up. He is more and more precious to us.

We also learned important lessons about God's providence. We attended a conference where the preacher talked about how Christians sometimes find themselves in a box of circumstances which they would never have chosen. Nevertheless, we're called to trust Him and to be faithful to Him in that box of circumstances. The challenge of that helped us to stay strong over the coming months.

The months continued to tick by. In November, a month before our baby was due, Jennie's grandfather died at the age of ninety-eight. In lots of ways, he'd been the glue which had held Jennie's dad's side of the family together. Even today, the whole family remembers him with affection.

In the end, it was decided that our baby should be born by caesarean section on 6 December at the hospital an hour away. It was possible that some of her spinal tissue might be exposed through the lesion in her back and the hospital felt that a caesarean was therefore the best way to deliver her safely and quickly.

And so 6 December arrived. It had been hard to cope with all the love we'd received at church the previous day. And at 7 a.m., we took that hour's journey along the busy road to the hospital. We prayed that our baby would come out kicking and screaming; after all, it was by no means certain that she would be able to breathe, let alone move her legs. As we parked up, we had no idea how things were going to turn out from here.

5

The First Six Months

Going in for an elective caesarean is a strange experience. You go in, you have your baby and you have lunch. At least, that's what it's like for the father.

We arrived at the hospital early in the morning of 6 December. We checked in and, after what seemed like an eternity, Jennie was whisked away to be prepared for the delivery. James was left alone in a room – where eventually a midwife remembered him and came to collect him just as the procedure was about to begin.

We'd printed out Psalm 18:1-6 and taken it with us into the theatre. The Psalmist, David, writes, 'I love you, Lord, my strength. The Lord is my rock, my fortress, and my deliverer, my God, my rock where I seek refuge, my shield and the horn of my salvation, my stronghold. I called to the Lord, who is worthy of praise, and I was saved from my enemies. The ropes of death were wrapped around me; the torrents of destruction terrified me. The ropes of Sheol entangled me; the snares of death confronted me. I called to the Lord in my distress, and I cried to my God for help. From his temple he heard my voice, and my cry to him reached his ears.' If ever we needed Him to be our strength, our rock, our fortress, our deliverer, our refuge, our shield, our salvation and our stronghold, it was then.

At 10:59 a.m., our baby girl was born. We'd already decided to call her Elyania, roughly the Hebrew for 'God has answered'. And, just as we'd prayed, she came out kicking and screaming. There was a thin layer of skin over her lesion, giving some protection to the neural tissue which was exposed there. The staff weighed her, wrapped her up, and handed her to us.

It was a jubilant but surreal moment. All that waiting, all those scans... And now we were holding Elly in our arms as the staff were congratulating us! There she was this precious little gift who already looked like a mini-Jennie! We felt extreme joy. We felt an overwhelming calmness. We were thrilled to see that she could move her legs. Our hearts pounded with love for her.

And then reality kicked in again. They needed to take Elly away to check her out more thoroughly. Jennie longed for James to stay with her as they stitched up her wound, but was desperate for Elly not to be alone without a parent so sent James on his way to be with her. It was a little taste of the sacrifice which goes along with parenthood. We were all reunited a couple of hours later while Jennie was still in recovery.

Over the next 24 hours, the thin layer of skin covering Elly's lesion ruptured, leaving things exposed. Spinal cerebral fluid started to leak out from it, giving a high risk of meningitis. So it was decided that on the second day of her life, she should have massive spinal surgery to repair the lesion. The surgeons gathered and explained the risks, which were substantial. It was possible that she would lose the control she had over her legs and over her bladder and bowels. But the risk of doing nothing was far greater.

Again our church mobilized to pray for her two days later on 8 December during the operation, which took hours. Eventually she was returned to the Special Care Baby Unit in an incubator, looking so incredibly vulnerable and so cute all at the same time.

It's a strange feeling for a parent to see your child so helpless. All of our parenting instincts are to protect, to provide, to support, to nurture, but at that moment, all we could do was watch and pray. And wait. Again.

The following day, the neuro-surgeons visited and were very pleased with Elly's progress. She was still able to move her legs, though nobody could tell whether that was going to translate into the ability to walk later on in life.

When you're caring for someone in hospital, life takes on a strange rhythm. There are hours of sitting. There are the regular medical observations. There are the daily visits from the surgical team. It's a peculiar existence as you'll know if you've been there. During that time, we were taught how to catheterize

Elly because her bladder was never fully emptying. We were taught how to give her the medication she'd need at home. And we started to learn how to do parenting in general.

After a little under a fortnight, we were discharged and went home. To be away from all the medical staff who were on hand to answer our every question was unsettling. And it was snowing. Strangely it was also Elly's first experience of daylight, having been in a womb or a hospital until then. In those early days, we would go back to the hospital every two or three days for them to check Elly out. Within a couple of weeks, though, it was clear that the operation had gone as well as it could have done and that Elly had made a very good recovery.

What took priority now was her hydrocephalus. Cerebrospinal fluid, CSF, started to build up inside her skull, which for many reasons was not good. There was the danger of her brain being compressed by the pressure of this extra fluid. There was the danger of her head growing very large. There was even, ultimately, the danger of death. The neurosurgeons expected to carry out brain surgery to correct this at some point in the future, but they wanted to leave it until it was definitely necessary.

The technical equipment which the hospital provided so that we could monitor this was... a paper tape measure. Every two days we had to measure Elly's head to see whether it was growing abnormally. If it was, we were to report to the hospital immediately. There were other signs we had to look out for too, such as sunsetting eyes (eyes which can't look upwards), excessive sleepiness, and a bulging fontanelle (the squashy bit on a baby's head).

Now, this doesn't sound too stressful, but it was nerve-racking. Almost every moment of every day we were on the lookout for hydrocephalus. One day in January, Elly was blue-lighted to the hospital an hour away because her fontanelle was pulsating and because she'd slept for about twenty-one hours (which sounds quite nice, but in that condition, isn't). After examination, the neuro-surgeons felt they didn't need to operate just yet.

On other occasions, Elly would succumb to a more common illness and this too would push up the pressure in her head. We'd go to the hospital, they'd check her out, and they'd send us home.

In the end, despite all our attention, we missed the signs of hydrocephalus when they finally arrived. We had a routine appointment at the hospital. The neuro-surgical consultant took one look at her and booked her in for brain surgery the following week to fit a shunt. At the time we wrote this: 'When we heard yesterday that she needed the operation, we were both taken by surprise. We felt like we'd been turning right at traffic lights in our Nissan Micra only to be hit from the side by another car. We really hadn't seen it coming. James was preaching on Sunday night, though, about how God is in control even of the details of our lives, and we believe that with all our hearts. We know that His hand is upon us, and we trust Him to help us as we look another trying week in the face.'

And his hand was upon us in two special ways.

First, the operation went very well. Prior to the day of surgery, Elly had an MRI scan in the middle of the night. The surgeons concluded that she didn't need a shunt after all; instead they wanted to carry out an endoscopic third ventriculostomy. This is where a tiny hole is made in the floor of the third ventricle of the brain to allow the CSF to flow rather than build up. It took another two months of anxious waiting, but the procedure was a complete success. Even up to the time of writing, it hasn't gone wrong, nor is it expected to.

The second way in which we felt God's hand in control was totally unforeseen. On the night before Elly's brain surgery, one of the surgeons had been waiting for us to be admitted to have a chat with us. He told us that his own wife was expecting a baby and that they'd had a very worrying 20-week scan. They'd been advised to go for an abortion. However, they'd chosen not to. And a large part of the reason was that he remembered Elly and conversations he'd had with us at the time of her birth. They were determined to go through with the pregnancy, no matter what the outcome might be. He was waiting to thank us.

And that was staggeringly precious to us. To know that our little girl was a life-saver, even at the age of five months! We were so grateful to God for that token of His goodness to us and for the opportunity to use our difficulties for Him. Hearing that the night before her surgery gave us a sense of joy the following day at a time which should have been anything but joyful.

From then, life with Elly started to become a bit more normal. It was a very new normal for us. And it wasn't very normal compared to other families.

But while all of this had been happening, there had been some other tragic events in our close family. And that's where our story turns now...

6

Bev

Rewind a little. It was February 2010, two months before we knew Elly was on the way. Jennie was working in the office. She was normally on house calls in the community but she'd deliberately kept her diary free to be doing admin all day so she was ready to take that call.

Her mother, Bev, had been unwell for a while. She'd had litres of ascitic fluid drained from her abdomen, which we all knew was very suspicious. In our hearts, we knew what was going on but there had been no confirmation. That morning she had an appointment with the oncologist. She'd had cancer before and battled it well with God's help and had been in remission and clear for eight years.

The call came. Jennie grabbed the phone and went to a quiet corner. 'I'm just back from the hospital with Dad,' Bev said. 'They've confirmed it's cancer. It's terminal but you've still got me for a while.' 'How long?' Jennie gasped. 'Maybe a year.' Jennie was stunned. She'd battled it before; surely she could battle it again.

'How long?' Jennie asked again in disbelief. 'A year. You've still got me for a year,' she said with a jokey sarcasm. And then Jennie cried. Bev had always seemed so strong: she was a tough, resilient, vocal Aussie. 'Don't,' she said. 'It's OK.' They chatted a little more, talking about treatment plans and then about how everyone in the family was, which seemed banal compared to the news Bev had just shared.

With that phone call the world somehow changed. Someone Jennie could always rely on was, some day soon, going to be no more. This was now reality.

Jennie went to the toilet and composed herself. With a heavy heart she went back into the office. She saw her boss and cried. 'That was my mum on the phone,' she said. 'She's got cancer and it's....'

'Go!' her boss said. 'Go home! You don't need to be here now!'

There then followed lots of hospital visits. Jennie went to visit when she could or when her dad, Bob, needed support. And in those early days Bev went downhill quite quickly. The whole family was alarmed. Jennie's sister, Pam, was living in Australia at the time of the diagnosis and decided it was right to come back to the UK to be around their mum to make the most of the time.

Two months later it was a great joy for Jennie to tell her mum that we were expecting a baby. This would be her first grandchild. The news was instantly a distraction from the sadness and pain for everyone. A wave of hope and excitement broke on everyone's minds. A happiness descended into the gloom. Bev hadn't expected to have grandchildren let alone to see one!

There was now a greater urgency about doing things together as a family. It was exciting for Jennie to be able to go shopping for some maternity clothes with her mum and sister. When there weren't any that were suitable, Bev was disappointed as she'd wanted to buy a special dress for Jennie. The disappointment was soon overcome when, next week, Pam dropped in and handed over three or four dresses they'd found together. One of these dresses Jennie has kept as a precious memory.

Bob cherished the time he had remaining with Bev. He took her out whenever he could often for drives in the country. He learnt how to do things he'd not done before, like the shopping and making beds for family who were visiting. He arranged for the bathroom to be redesigned and decorated so Bev would be able to use it when she was weaker. They had a special holiday together.

In the summer, Jennie's Uncle Mal, took long-service leave from his firm in Australia and came over to be with Bev for the whole summer. This gave her a huge boost. They chatted over old times together. They went to local coffee shops together (a lot!). It was great to see them together. She was obviously very tired but was determined to make the most of every moment. It was during this time that Elly's diagnosis was given.

You'll remember from Chapter Three that once we'd heard a provisional diagnosis of spina bifida we immediately called our parents. On that initial call, Bev was calm and relayed details about babies she'd looked after with spina bifida. When we called again on the Monday after the diagnosis had been confirmed, her response then shook Jennie to the core. Bev cried. Nor was it normal crying. It was a shrill, ear-piercing cry, so much so that she dropped the phone and Pam had to take over. She never cried, let alone like this! As time went by we understood that the contrasting emotions of it all – her excitement at being a grandmother and her sadness for our situation – were just too much for her to bear.

Bev was determined to spend time with us and we arranged for her to come to stay for a week. She and Jennie had a very special time together. They too went to coffee shops (a lot!). They went on boat trips. They talked. They went shopping together. She cooked for us when she was able. In that week, when we were out and about, there seemed to be an unusually high number of people commenting on the baby bump. Somehow the conversation always got round to the baby's diagnosis. Bev would sit and listen and Jennie later learned that she was proud of those conversations. The way she'd handled them had given her confidence that we weren't going to fall apart.

When the time came for Uncle Mal to return to Australia it was a very emotional and poignant parting. It was hard to see him waving goodbye to Bev. It would be the last time he would ever see her and everyone was well aware of that.

We had wanted to do something as a wider family. If Bev had had a bucket list, one item on it would have been to go to the Edinburgh Military Tattoo and to stay in a posh hotel whilst doing so. We booked the tickets and all went up on the train together. We were driven very close to the door of Edinburgh Castle so she didn't need to walk far. She managed well and the evening was very special with many tears from everyone. There were songs which brought back memories for Bev and she regaled us with her stories. She seemed so pleased that she'd achieved this lifelong ambition despite being so ill.

The months rolled on. In December, the day before Elly was going to be born, Jennie's sister visited their mum. It was Sunday and that afternoon Pam called Jennie to say that their mum had gone downhill rapidly. That was the straw that broke the camel's back. Jennie had coped with church OK on the Sunday morning and had held it together. But after getting that call, she was in no state to manage going to the evening service. We stayed home with much anxiety and weeping about what was to come for ourselves, for Elly, and for Bev.

When Elly was born the next day, James rang the family. Bev was so excited. Jennie spoke to her later on that day and she was eager to hear about everything. She was too ill to travel and Jennie's dad needed to stay with her. We could hear the anguish in her voice as she was desperate to meet Elly. When Pam came to visit she brought presents from them. Bev had picked some of them out herself which had personalized names on. Things like this still mean a lot to us.

We had expected to stay in hospital until well after Christmas following Elly's birth. As a result the wider family had made no plans for Christmas – everything was just in a state of suspended animation. It was so special when we received the news from a nurse that we could go home – eight days before Christmas. We rang Bev excitedly and she was thrilled. 'So I get to see Elly!' she exclaimed joyfully. 'Yes,' Jennie said. 'We're going to come to stay for Christmas! And whilst we're there, can you give Elly her first proper bath?' She was thrilled.

Christmas was special... and tiring. We also saw the New Year in with her. It was a time of year she loved; again, there were more memories for everyone.

But as 2011 started it was clear that Bev was declining quite rapidly again. We all knew when last February's 'maybe a year' was up. We visited whenever we could, which often meant late-night travelling with a young baby. There were numerous times when we had to stop in car parks or lay-bys to feed a screaming baby. We had a contraption which played music and projected a light show onto the roof of the car: we heard those tunes so often that even today we can hear them in our heads!

Bev was due to be seventy on 1 March 2011. We planned a special birthday meal and a canal boat trip about a week later. The boat company had somehow got wind of how ill Bev was and agreed to pay for the trip with a local paper coming along to take some photos. She made it to her birthday meal but was unable to come downstairs: she was too weak in bed. We took her birthday cake up to her. She never made the boat trip.

At 6 o'clock in the morning on 17 March 2011, with Elly just over three months old, the phone rang. James answered. It was Pam. What she said was very simple and agonisingly difficult to hear. 'I've just spoken to the doctor. Mum's not got long.'

Jennie jumped out of bed. She put on some clothes, threw some things in the car and set off on the two-and-a-half hour journey. She didn't stop until she suddenly realized that she hadn't had any breakfast and that the car was about to run out of petrol.

When Jennie got to the hospital, Bev was still just about able to speak. She smiled. One by one, all the family arrived. James arrived with Elly about three hours after Jennie. Bev was thrilled to see her and managed to raise an arm to stroke her head. The whole family went to the bedside one by one, and Bev held our hands.

Throughout the day Bev gradually slipped away. She died about 8 o'clock that evening. She ended her journey well. She lived and breathed Christ. She constantly told people about Him. She wanted to be with Him. And she held fast to Him in her last days and hours.

What is grief? We had already started to grieve before Bev died knowing what was going to happen. We'd also experienced grief in other situations of loss. But now we, and especially Jennie, entered into a far deeper experience of grief than we'd ever known before. Her mum was not here any more.

There were things which took the edge off the misery. Jennie was so pleased that her mum had seen and held a grandchild and Bev herself had been thrilled. Heaven started to take on a new meaning. We were pleased for her to be there. We were pleased that we'd had a chance to say goodbye and a good year of memories with her following the prognosis; there are so many who don't get that time.

At the same time we were so sad to have lost her. Jennie was desperate for motherly advice on parenting. She was desperate to have a motherly hug. She was desperate to ask those questions that she couldn't ask anyone else. She was desperate to see her pride as she watched Elly grow and achieve so much. She just missed her. But now... she wasn't there.

Funeral plans were made and the service was a joyous occasion. Jennie's Uncle Mal made the journey over from Australia again, and his support was tremendous. The following weeks and months were a haze as we sought to support each other in the family and to spend time together. Life went on, but grief continued on too. Life was never the same for Jennie or the family. Our experience so far is that you never truly get over the loss of losing someone so close; you just learn new ways of coping and living.

7

Sam

When Elly was born, James's brother, Samuel, was twenty-six. He was born with Down's Syndrome. And as a result of that, he quickly became the focal point of James's family's life. Everybody loved him. He got away with all kinds of things which his parents would never have let James and his sister get away with.

As he went through life, Sam spent more years in full-time academic study than any other Muldoon in history. He attended his local primary school with a teaching assistant helping him. He went to a special secondary school. And then he took various courses at colleges local to him.

Sam had an incredible memory. He memorized entire scripts of Laurel and Hardy films. If you quoted the first line of a hymn, he would be able to tell you what number it was in the hymn book. He liked to be able to say hello in as many different languages as he could.

Sam was a Christian. We're not sure exactly when he put his faith in the Lord Jesus Christ. Nor would he have been able necessarily to have given you a full account of the gospel. But it was abundantly clear that he trusted Jesus and that he loved Him. He enjoyed reading an easy-English Bible and church was the highlight of his week. One of the greatest joys of Muldoon family life was the night he was baptized at his local church.

In early 2011, a couple of months after Elly's birth and while we were still getting our heads round Bev's terminal condition, Sam started to get unwell. He was languid and sluggish and found it hard to motivate himself to do anything. James's parents noted that his breathing rate was very fast when he was in bed and found that his heart-rate was elevated. A number of tests were carried out, but nobody could figure out what was going on.

In early March Sam had a blood test. A few days later, on 11 March, just six days before Bev went to be with the Lord, the doctor unexpectedly came to the house to talk to Sam and his parents about the results. It can never be a good thing for the doctor to come round to your house unexpectedly to do that. And it wasn't. They'd discovered that Sam had acute lymphoblastic leukaemia.

From that moment, our lives, and particularly the lives of James's parents, were never the same again. Within a few hours, Sam had been rushed an hour up the road to the closest specialist hospital. He'd been booked in for a bone marrow biopsy and for chemotherapy to start the following week. The entire family was left reeling and James's parents were left utterly bewildered. One of our abiding memories of that day is seeing Sam and his dad, looking completely lost, riding off in the ambulance together facing... who knew what?

Chemo was awful for Sam. The hospital staff decided to shave his head, knowing that he was certain to lose his hair. He was very unwell with the side effects of the treatment. Having completed that particular course of chemo he moved on to radiotherapy to try to obliterate any vestiges of the leukaemia which had been left in particular parts of his body.

All of this was happening about an hour's drive away from his home in the Fens. James's parents as good as moved into the hospital so that they could be with him. One of them would often sleep (or not sleep) in a chair by his bed. James's sister, Mo, would visit as often as she could. We would visit too, though generally Elly wasn't allowed into Sam's hospital room so as to avoid him picking up an infection from her.

All in all, those months were gruelling in the extreme. There were times when we thought we were going to lose Sam. There were times when he was doing a bit better. We prayed and feared and lamented and agonized and prayed some more. And yet Sam took everything very bravely and without complaining. We could see the grace of God at work in his life. And, sure enough, he was soon in remission. He was able to come home for much of the summer of 2011. And life was even somewhat normal.

During September, however, Sam started to get ill again. By the start of October he was sent back to the specialist hospital an hour away. They planned to carry out various tests but, in the end, a blood test was all they really needed. His leukaemia had returned aggressively. His body was not going to be able to cope with chemotherapy again so they switched him to palliative care.

This was obviously a terrible blow, especially to James's parents. They'd invested so much of their lives in him and carrying on without him was almost impossible to contemplate. Nevertheless none of us doubted that the Lord was with us in every circumstance.

When he started palliative care, Sam immediately started to feel better. He started eating more normally and showing more interest in life. He was able to return home. He and James's parents were able to get out and about a lot, even managing a day trip to Mablethorpe, that 'lovely' east coast seaside town which Sam had loved to visit, mainly because he'd been indoctrinated into doing so by James's dad. They were bittersweet times.

In November that year, nine months after he was diagnosed, Sam caught an infection, and, given that his leukaemia had destroyed his immune system, he was soon back in hospital again. He was transferred to hospice care within a hospital in a magnificently flat Fenland town near home, which was much easier for James's parents; they were both with him during the day and one of them could go home during the night whilst the other stayed with Sam. Strong fellow that he was, he fought on for several more weeks.

6 December was Elly's first birthday. We remember taking her to the hospital to see Sam. She wasn't allowed to go into his room, but she waved to him from the doorway. She also shared some of her birthday cake with him!

On 18 December, James was preparing to preach at a Christmas family service. And it was then that he received the call he'd been dreading. It was the hospital. Sam had enjoyed himself at a carol service put on by some local children the day before, but he'd suddenly gone into decline, his poor body weakened beyond its ability to continue.

Within a few minutes James had set off, a dreadful sinking feeling within. In the event, he'd hardly reached the motorway before he heard that Sam had died. It had been very peaceful. There had been family with him. James, Mo and their parents gathered a short while afterwards around Sam's dead body; they stood there broken, and yet assured that his spirit was now well and truly alive in the presence of his Saviour.

Hundreds of people came to Sam's funeral a couple of weeks later. We grieved. We laughed. We celebrated God's goodness to us in giving us Sam. And then we tried to start to live life without him. We'd already learned a lot about grief through losing Bev nine months earlier. Now we were having to learn new lessons all over again. In fact, James's experience of grief in the loss of his brother was quite different from Jennie's experience of grief in the loss of her mother. And that's not surprising. When you face grief, there are many different factors involved in how it feels to you: your own personality, the nature of your relationship with the one who has died, the vitality of your relationship with the one who has died, and so on. There's no telling how grief is actually going to feel until it strikes you.

As people who have lost loved ones know, you never get over the sense of loss. Life goes on but with a gaping chasm inside. And it was very hard to start to live without Sam. James's parents had the intense grief of living life with the loss of their son; what parent ever expects that? But they also had dozens of hours each week to fill. So much of their time had revolved around caring for Sam, especially in that last year of his life. Now there was the emptiness of heart and emptiness of time to cope with. In a very real sense, there was a loss of identity with the loss of their son. And that was not easy to bear at all. For James's mum especially, the first year was appalling. But the second year was even worse – such is the unpredictable course of grief.

Since then James's parents have gradually started to reconstruct their lives from the rubble left by their bereavement. But never a day goes by when Sam is not there in some way, shape or form.

In the end, the only hope we had as a family was the hope of heaven. Heaven had been very precious to us in the wake of losing Bev. Now it became very precious to us again. We knew that Sam's spirit was there, at home with the Lord. We knew that one day, his body would be raised and that he would be part of that new creation. It was a strange thought to think of him as perfected, as delivered from Down's Syndrome, in that recreated universe, and it still is a strange thought. But we'll see him there – and sometimes that's the only thing which has kept us going.

In the face of all this – Elly's disabilities, the loss of Bev, the loss of Sam – here's what we wrote in our Christmas newsletter at the end of 2011: 'So that's where we are. The apostle Paul once wrote about being "hard pressed on every side, but not crushed; perplexed, but not in despair" in 2 Corinthians 4:8. We've often felt the same way. But we know that it's God's grace which has kept us going.' We were on our knees in all kinds of ways. And we were praying that 2012 would be rather more straightforward.

Which leads us to the last chapter of our story...

8

Attrition

By the start of 2012, we were praying for one thing: for a calmer year. And that's how it turned out. There were no major crises. There were lots of hospital visits with Elly, but they were all routine. Nobody in our families died. We'd really felt that the smell of death was attached to us and that everywhere we went people were likely to be doomed, but 2012 was a bit of an oasis in the midst of all our trials.

That's not to say that it was all easy. The big question of the year was: would Elly walk? Most children start walking some time after their first birthday, though there are always children who walk sooner and children who walk later. We were wondering whether Elly would walk at all.

As Elly was approaching her second birthday, she hadn't started to walk. She'd stubbornly refused to adopt the toddler equivalent of a zimmer frame which would have helped her. Our physiotherapist was talking increasingly about wheelchairs. And then, almost out of nowhere, in the middle of a physio session, she suddenly just got up and walked. Our physiotherapist cried almost as much as Jennie did!

Since then, there have been many ups and downs in life. There have been great highs, such as the birth of our second daughter, Livia (Livvy), in 2013; and the birth of our son, Nathaniel (Nate), in 2016. But there have also been more trials.

In 2015 Elly contracted meningitis. She became gradually more and more ill and, despite visits to multiple hospitals, nobody could find out what was going on. Finally, on the day we were due to go on holiday, they worked out that she'd got meningitis.

She was desperately ill. She spent the best part of three days sleeping or whimpering before the intravenous antibiotics kicked in. And then, by God's grace, she started to get better. It was weeks before she could eat normally and she lost 10 per cent of her body weight over that time. In the end, remarkably, she made a full recovery.

Then in early 2017 James's sister, Mo, was diagnosed with cancer. She'd had virtually no symptoms at all, and by the time it was detected it had spread to many different parts of her body. To begin with it looked likely that she would have only a few months to live. It was just over five years since we'd lost Sam, and this devastated the entire family once again.

Since then, Mo has been under continual medication and has coped with it heroically. Her cancer has been largely held back by the gruelling treatment she's had. We keep on praying for her.

Just before Easter 2017 Nate, then five months old, contracted sepsis. He caught chickenpox before his immune system was strong, the spots drew a bacterial infection into his blood, and before long he was very unwell. We've never seen anyone looking as ill as Nate did then.

This time, his condition was diagnosed very quickly and treatment was started through a cannula in his head – the only place on his body which wasn't too podgy to be able to find a blood vessel! He recovered – but it was over a year before he let us out of his sight again.

By the time Nate started to get over his sepsis, we found that we were very, very weary. And as the weeks went by, Jennie couldn't shake that weariness. She was relentlessly tired, and it was not at all clear what was going on with her. In our confusion we prayed, we sought support from the leaders of the church and we consulted various doctors and counsellors. In the end, the conclusion was that Jennie was suffering from burnout.

The way we explained it at the time was this. Jennie might normally have had 500 units of energy per day. Doing the school run might use 20 units. Leading a meeting at church might use 70 units. Keeping James in order might use 100 units (at least). But it was as though she was starting, not with 500 units of energy, but with 50. Therefore even the most moderate tasks were exhausting her. Each day was filled with frustration and exasperation, a desire to live normally but an inability to do so.

One of the things we realized off the back of this is how attritional it is caring for someone with a disability or living with a disability. At the time of writing, Elly is still doing brilliantly. But she's increasingly self-aware and we have many deep conversations with her as a result. Each day we have to spend between one and three hours caring for her medical needs.

Actually, the effects on James were different. The way it revealed itself in him was that he became emotionally lifeless. It wasn't that he was depressed, because he wasn't. It wasn't that he didn't like what he was doing in life, because he did. It's just that he became unable to feel much joy or much pain.

One night in particular brought this to light. Jennie woke James at 2 a.m. one morning in spring 2018 in extreme pain. She really thought she was going to die. The ambulance came and took her into the local hospital where, with a mixture of pain-killing drugs, the pain receded. Jennie slept for much of the next week. Two months later, gall stones were diagnosed. Through all of this, James felt very little, something which just wasn't normal.

The crises and the attrition had taken its toll on both of us but in different ways. We're still learning how to cope with this, but there are three things which we know have helped especially.

First, friends. We've both, but Jennie in particular, found it helpful to have friends who have been ready to give us time and who have been ready to listen to us. There aren't too many people who have been able to offer us both time and ears. But those who have, have made a massive difference to us. To be understood, to have our pain validated, to be reminded that we have been through a lot – all of this has helped us. We're very grateful to God for the people He has sent our way to support us and to bear our burdens with us.

Second, time. James's church have three times relieved James of his normal duties to be able to give more time to situations at home. Without this, we would not have been able to keep going in the long run. It's been hard at times for the church leaders to know how best to support us, but when they've given us that extra time, it's led to a measure of recovery for us both.

Third, grace. At the end of last year, we wrote: 'The attrition … and the traumas and bereavements of the last seven years have taken their toll. Nevertheless, we thoroughly believe the truth of Psalm 119:68 which, talking about the Lord, says, "You are good, and you do what is good".' His grace has never let us go. It is not letting us go now. And it will never let us go. But we have had to learn that the hard way.

In the past we sometimes used to tell people that the Lord will not call us to go through situations which are too much for us to bear. I suppose we misunderstood verses such as 1 Corinthians 10:13 which says, 'No temptation has come upon you except what is common to humanity. But God is faithful; he will not allow you to be tempted beyond what you are able, but with the temptation he will also provide a way out so that you may be able to bear it.' We have been through situations which are too much for us to bear. What we now say is that the Lord will not call us to go through situations which are too much for Him to carry us through. We've learned, in our hardest times, in our neediest times, that He is just as much at the bottom of the pit as He is as the top of the mountain. And for that, we are so very grateful.

Our own experiences have also taught us a great deal about how to support others in situations of suffering, and that is where we're turning now.

Part II – Introduction

That brings us to Part Two. And in Part Two we list seven of the lessons we've learned about supporting people who are suffering. We hope these will be helpful to you as you seek to support others.

Sometimes suffering can be a very private thing. Perhaps because of the personalities of those suffering or because of the nature of the suffering itself – maybe because there are problems in a marriage or with other close family members – nobody else is welcome to be involved in giving support. But where you have friends who are ready to accept help from you, we want to equip you to make a start. This book is not intended to be a Seven-Steps-To-Help-Your-Suffering-Friends-Infallibly guide. We simply want to give you a few ideas about how you could best support others in their times of need.

And that's important. While we were in the process of writing this book, we happened to see an interview on BBC Breakfast

News where a lady was discussing the importance of peer support when times are tough. She made the very simple point that often people do not support the suffering because they don't know what to do. They're nervous of saying or doing the wrong thing. They're worried that they'll get out of their depth. They don't want to interfere where they may not be wanted. Far safer, then, just to keep away and to leave the care to the 'professionals', whoever they might be.

We've found over the years that that is true. People can shy away from those who are suffering because they're just plain scared. They often want to help but they haven't got a clue how to do it.

So the point of this part of our self-consciously brief book is to give you a bit of help just to get off the ground. We're going to be very practical, even challenging some of the time. But what we want to do is to show you that you, as one of God's people, can help your friends who are under the very real pressure of suffering. We're called as Christians to be family to one another and we want to equip you to start to be confident enough to take the risk of getting involved with others in their tough times.

As we've written the next seven chapters, we've often found ourselves being challenged by what we've written. As we come alongside others, we don't always get it right. We don't always live up to what we're about to say. We make mistakes. We sometimes get home after time with suffering friends and beat ourselves up (metaphorically). We get it wrong. We're not perfect.

But not being perfect is OK, and as long as, in the end, we are pointing people to the One who is perfect, we'll have done something of use. So please don't think of us as perfect counsellors and helpers. We're not – and if you know us, you'll know that already! But, relying on God's sustaining and forgiving grace, we are all called to play our part. In Part Two we want to encourage you to get on with the privilege of helping the suffering.

9

The Bible Helps

The first thing we've learned about helping the suffering from what we've been through is this: the Bible helps.

That, of course, is a perfectly obvious lesson. We can imagine you nodding sagely in agreement with us as you dip your digestive into your cup of tea. Of course, the Bible helps! It's the word of God.

The thing is: often we forget the power of the word of God. Just think about Deuteronomy 8:3 for a moment. At the end of the verse, Moses says that the Lord wanted to teach the Israelites that 'man does not live on bread alone but on every word that comes from the mouth of the Lord'.

The implications of those words are striking. They teach us that people are dead without the word of God, just as people without food end up dead. They teach that Christians are listless without the word of God, just as people who are physically malnourished are listless. They teach that Christians revive when they hear the word of God, just as hungry people revive when they start to eat again. And, given the fact that these words are quoted by Jesus in Matthew 4:4 at a time when He's being tempted by the devil, they teach that the word of God arms us to face the enemy. The Bible does all that. There's power there, isn't there? Christians who fail to take the Bible seriously end up spiritually famished and atrophied.

We need the Bible every day of our lives, but there are times when we especially need the sustenance which can come only from it. One of those times is when we suffer.

So we're grateful to people who contacted us through our ordeals and quoted Bible verses to us. Here are just a few of the verses which people sent us which helped us.

> Do not fear, for I am with you; do not be afraid, for I am your God. I will strengthen you; I will help you; I will hold on to you with my righteous right hand (Isa. 41:10).

> This I know: God is for me (Ps. 56:9).

> The God of old is your dwelling place, and underneath are the everlasting arms (Deut. 33:27).

> And my God will supply all your needs according to his riches in glory in Christ Jesus (Phil. 4:19).

We're so glad that people took the time to think of verses to share with us. Many people did not share verses; they supported us in other ways. But those Bible passages helped. The word of God helps.

There were times, in fact, when it was only the word of God which kept us going. When we were telling our story in Part One, we mentioned that night when James broke down because it suddenly dawned on him that he'd taken time off to decorate a room for someone who might not live to use it. Yet at the same time he felt overwhelmed by a sense of God's goodness and control. That overwhelming sense of God's goodness and control came through the word of God. He remembered Psalm 62:11-12. 'God has spoken once; I have heard this twice: strength belongs to God, and faithful love belongs to you, Lord. For you repay each according to his works.' And there it was! God was strong, God was loving, and therefore we were safe. Even if the very worst happened, we were safe.

A verse Jennie has kept returning to throughout everything has been Psalm 119:68. 'You are good, and you do what is good,' it says. No matter what happened, the good God would be good to us.

Sometimes, in fact, the word of God has come to us in surprising ways and through unexpected people. When our second daughter, Livvy, was one year old, she went to a routine doctor's appointment at the hospital for something to do with her weight. The night before she'd had a bit of a sore eye; we thought she'd rubbed something into it and didn't think too much of it. But as soon as the doctor saw her, she said, 'We're not going to talk about her weight today; that eye needs sorting now. This is very serious and if it isn't sorted now, she could go blind. I'm going to admit her.' She diagnosed orbital cellulitis and before we knew it, Livvy was on intravenous antibiotics.

Naturally, we were upset. Then just as we were in the midst of all that emotion, Elly, who was three at the time, suddenly broke into song. She sang...

> Be strong and courageous
> The Lord of the Ages
> Holds all his little ones
> Safe by his side.
> Be strong and courageous
> The Lord of the Ages
> Holds all his little ones safe.[1]

It's a song by the Australian musician Colin Buchanan and it picks up on words from Joshua 1:9 where the Lord encourages His servant Joshua that he is going to lead the people of Israel into the Promised Land. It was God's word coming to us in a surprising way through an unexpected person, and the Lord used it to give us peace in all the turbulence of what we were going through. It changed our perspective entirely.

The word of God helps. We've sought to remember that as we've come alongside others in situations of suffering. Sometimes the word of God will be like a chink of light shining through extreme darkness. Sometimes it will provide the spiritual calories required to get someone spiritually refreshed and energized again.

---

1   'Be strong and Courageous', Colin Buchanan, 2004.

And the word of God is something which you could use to help others who are suffering, isn't it?

Let's say you're going to visit a friend whose husband has been unfaithful to her. What could you do on that visit? You could talk with her. You could weep with her. You could get angry at the suffering which has been inflicted upon her. You could give her some practical support. You could help her to think through some of the tough decisions she has to make. You could pray with her. And all that would be great.

But you could also share something from the Bible with her. Why not think in advance of your visit about a passage which will help her? Maybe before you go you could search your Bible for something relevant. If you're really stuck you could use an online Bible or a reference book. Go with the word of God. Share it with her. Because the word of God helps.

And that applies to all kinds of situations of suffering. What could you share with someone who is ill? Or with someone whose children have just left home? Or with someone who has lost his wife? Or with someone who has just been made redundant? Or with a couple who are struggling with infertility? Or with a friend who is struggling with unwanted singleness? Or with someone who is in debt and who can't see a way out? Or with someone who is being bullied at school? Think about Bible passages you could read with them or message them or even send to them in a card. You could do that, couldn't you?

We do just need to add one word of caution here: it's possible to misuse the Bible. For example, it can be easy to take verses out of context and to apply them in ways in which they should not be applied. Just be aware of that.

It's also possible to use the Bible in a thoughtless kind of way. Years ago, we had a slightly eccentric Christian friend. Most people have one of those! One day our friend told us about a time when he was driving somewhere in the south of England. He had his wife with him, and there was an elderly lady in the back seat of his car. We don't remember how it happened, but they were involved in an accident which was severe enough for the fire brigade to be called.

Our friend and his wife were able to get out of the car more-or-less unscathed. The elderly lady in the back, however, was trapped in the car and the fire brigade had to cut her out. She wasn't too badly injured as it turned out, but she was stuck in there. And our friend said to us, 'As the fire brigade were cutting her out of the car, I quoted Romans 8:28 to her: "All things work together for good..." She didn't seem very impressed with that!'

That is not a great use of the Bible. As you're being cut out of a vehicle, you're probably not ready to hear about all the good the Lord is going to accomplish in your life through what you're suffering. You're probably more focused on just getting out of there. We've come across many other examples of encouraging verses like that being used in glib or ill-timed ways, so robbing them of their power.

So do think carefully about the verses you use, but do use them. Don't shy away from quoting the Bible to people. It's living and active. It's penetrating. It's refreshing and reviving. And the Lord can really use you as you quote His words to minister His grace into the lives of your suffering friends.

The word of God helps. So make the most of it.

10

Prayer Helps

The second thing we've learned about helping the suffering is this: prayer helps.

That too, of course, is a perfectly obvious lesson. If you're reading straight on from the chapter before, you probably don't need another cup of tea to dip another digestive into. But we're sure you'll agree that prayer helps.

At least you do in your mind. Sometimes in our hearts, however, we're not so convinced. Praying seems, well, kind of futile. Does it really help? Does it make any difference at all? Isn't praying what you do when you can't do anything a bit more practical?

There are many Bible passages which challenge that heart attitude, but let's look at just one from the Old Testament, one which you may be less familiar with.

In Daniel 2, King Nebuchadnezzar, the King of Babylon, the mightiest man in the world, has a dream. Maybe at some time in your life you've had a dream which has really shaken you and you haven't been able to get it out of your mind. That was the sort of dream Nebuchadnezzar had. As a result of it he couldn't sleep and he couldn't concentrate. The mightiest man in the world reduced to a disturbed wreck... by a dream.

King Nebuchadnezzar calls in all the wise men of Babylon. He tells them that he's had a dream and that he wants them to interpret it. But there's a twist. So that he knows they're not pulling the wool over his eyes, he requires them to tell him the dream as well as the interpretation. If they fail, they'll be torn limb from limb and their houses will be turned into rubbish dumps.

The wise men are, of course, horrified. How can they possibly know what the king had dreamed about? They object. They stall. And in the end, Nebuchadnezzar is so infuriated that he orders the annihilation of all the wise men of Babylon. The problem is: that includes Daniel and his three friends who had been exiled with him from Judah.

What does Daniel do when Arioch, the chief executioner, comes to look for them? Daniel 2:17-18 tells us. 'Then Daniel went to his house and told his friends Hananiah, Mishael, and Azariah about the matter, urging them to ask the God of the heavens for mercy concerning this mystery, so Daniel and his friends would not be destroyed with the rest of Babylon's wise men.' What does he do? He gets people to pray for him. He explains the situation to his three friends and he asks them to ask God for mercy.

And why does he do that? Because he is thoroughly convinced that prayer helps! He doesn't get them to flee. He doesn't get them to make representations to the authorities. He doesn't get them to have a thought shower about what the king's dream might have been. He gets them to pray because he is thoroughly convinced that prayer helps.

And it does! God answers their prayers by revealing to Daniel in a vision the contents and the meaning of King Nebuchadnezzar's dream. Result: they and the wise men of Babylon are saved.

That, however, is a challenge to us. Yes, we pray but so often we do it without any kind of expectation that it's going to help at all. We pray because that's what Christians do. We pray because that's what's expected of us, but we don't really pray expecting God to answer. Or if He does, it will probably be a different sort of answer from the one we're looking for.

None of that is to say that God will always answer our prayers exactly as we ask them. He is much wiser than we are. He is much more loving that we are. He knows how to answer our prayers so that the best possible outcome arises in the best possible way. Nevertheless, He wants us to pray, He commands us to pray, and He will answer our prayers according to His will.

Throughout all the crises we've faced so far, people have prayed for us and we cannot express how thankful we are for that. And that prayer came in many different ways.

We had messages from people in all kinds of places who told us they were praying for us. Some of them were on the other side of the world and could not possibly help in a practical way. But they did help us: they told us that they prayed for us and they really did pray.

The church we belong to organized numerous prayer meetings for us, especially in the early days. Just after we shared about the diagnosis of Elly's spina bifida, a number of people from the church gathered to pray for us. During our normal church prayer meetings, there were often little slots just to pray for us. During particularly significant moments – such as when Elly was born or when she was having surgery – there were prayer meetings for us. It was an immense privilege to have people speaking to God on our behalf at those times.

We also had people come to pray with us. Individuals would sometimes visit us and pray with us. And groups of people would sometimes visit us and pray with us. Those times were often moving beyond words. For example, the elders of the church came over one night to pray with us for Elly before she was born, and we were blubbering wrecks throughout almost all of that meeting, yet we knew that we were together in God's presence and we knew that prayer helps.

We're thankful for all the prayers offered for us as a family and we're convinced that those prayers helped. God answered them. That we were kept sane, that we were kept close to each other, that Elly survived those early days, that Bev and Sam were upheld through their illnesses, that we were aware of

God's sheer faithfulness to us: all of those were answers to prayer. What a privilege to have a praying family! What an infinite privilege to have a God who hears and answers prayer.

And prayer is something which you could do to help others who are suffering, isn't it?

You're going to visit a friend who is in hospital waiting for surgery. It's a big operation. There's a possibility that she might lose her sight as a result of it, but if it goes well, it will make her life much more enjoyable for the years to come. You visit her. You chat with her. You hear her fears. You give her some reassurance. Please also pray with her. Even if you feel a little out of your comfort zone, pray with her. Even if it feels strange praying in a public space, pray with her. Because prayer helps.

And there are all kinds of things you can pray. You can pray for the operation to go perfectly. You can pray for recovery to go well. You can pray for peace. You can pray for God's everlasting arms to be felt around her. You can pray for her to be a good witness by what she's going through. You can pray for her family to be given a sense of calmness as they worry about her. You can listen carefully to her fears and pray with the words of relevant Bible promises about them. In advance of your visit, think about some things you could pray about. And then do it! Pray with her.

One of the great things about prayer, of course, is that you can do it at any time and in any place. So when you wake up in the night and remember your suffering friend, pray for her. When you're driving on the M4 and your friend comes to mind, pray for her (with your eyes open!) When her name comes up in conversation, shoot up a little prayer for her. Pray!

And please go on praying. People who are suffering keep on needing prayer, even when it might appear that the immediate crisis is over. We so appreciate the fact that some people have really understood our situation and keep on praying for us, even though we're not in a crisis situation at the moment. Prayer helps. So go on praying for the suffering. Add them to your prayer list or prayer app. Prayer helps.

And please, from time to time, keep on reminding those you know who are suffering that you are praying for them. Tell them what you're praying for and ask them if there are other things they'd really like you to be praying. To know that specific prayer is being offered is a tremendous encouragement and God delights to answer prayers like that according to His will.

So often in our praying, we're more like those people in Acts 12 than we are like Daniel in Daniel 2. The church prayed for Peter to be released from prison in Acts 12, but they didn't really expect that to happen. They were surprised when it did happen even when Peter started knocking on their door. In fact, they imagined every other possibility before they accepted that he really was there! Praise God – He may well answer prayers like that because He's merciful and kind.

Nevertheless, our prayers should be more Daniel 2-ish. Think big thoughts of God and then pray with and for your suffering friends. With faith. With confidence. With submission to God's greater wisdom and love. Because prayer helps.

11

Doctrine Helps

The third thing we've learned about helping the suffering is this: doctrine helps.

Doctrine? Seriously?

The idea that doctrine helps those who are suffering may sound odd to you. What does a woman need who's grieving the loss of her mother? A hug, perhaps. A card with some loving words. But doctrine? What does a man who's just lost his job need? Some money. Contacts. Doctrine?

It may sound odd. But we've sometimes found that doctrine has helped us more than almost anything else. Here are two examples.

When we first received the diagnosis that Elly was going to be born with spina bifida, we sent messages round to a number of our friends to ask them for prayer. People prayed and many of them also sent us messages. One was from some friends who had suffered the agony of miscarriage several times in the early years of their married life. They wrote.

> Guys. The church were praying a great deal for the three of you last night. I'm so sorry you've had this shock. I was reminded how fallen this world is, and how we often start to ignore and accept it until something upsetting happens. Your little girl is God's exquisite workmanship, yet her disabilities make us yearn all the more for the day we are given resurrection bodies in Christ.

And there's doctrine there. The world as we experience it today is under God's curse. There is suffering, there is groaning, there is a yearning for something better. You feel that every time you suffer something significant.

But it will not be like that forever. Jesus has come. He has absorbed the curse on our behalf. He has provided redemption, not merely for His people, but also for the cosmos, and one day, in one earth-shattering moment, the universe will be renewed. Every vestige of sin will be gone and every vestige of the stinging consequences of sin will be gone too. There will be new heavens and a new earth – and it will all be utterly perfect.

And knowing that helped us. The day is coming for us as people in Christ when suffering will be over. There will be no grieving over death then because there will be no death. There will be no more Down's Syndrome or spina bifida or attrition or burnout. There will be just joy – the sheer joy of being in the immediate presence of the Saviour in the perfect environment of His recreated world.

Knowing that helps. Being reminded of that helps. Doctrine helps.

Here's another example. Various aspects of the character of God have really helped us, in particular His power, His wisdom and His love. In fact, the combination of His power and wisdom and love has helped.

Imagine for a moment if God were wise and loving but not powerful. That wouldn't be enough, would it? He might be clever enough to know what we needed in any given situation, and He might be caring enough to want to make that happen. But if He were not also powerful, it would all be for nothing. He wouldn't be able to create the circumstances which could help us.

Imagine if He were wise and powerful but not loving. Again, it wouldn't be enough. God would know what to do, and He could do it – but He wouldn't care enough to make it happen.

And it also wouldn't be good enough if He were loving and powerful but not wise.

But the fact is: God is utterly wise. Think about 1 Corinthians 1:25: 'God's foolishness is wiser than human wisdom, and God's weakness is stronger than human strength.' God is wise enough to know what He's doing in any and every situation. He may not do what we expect. But He will do what is best.

And God is also utterly powerful. Think about Ephesians 3:20-1: 'Now to him who is able to do above and beyond all that we ask or think according to the power that works in us – to him be glory in the church and in Christ Jesus to all generations, forever and ever. Amen.' God is powerful enough to be able to help us in any and every situation. He may not do what we want. But nobody and nothing can thwart Him from doing whatever He chooses.

And God is also love. Think about 1 John 4:9-10: 'God's love was revealed among us in this way: God sent his one and only Son into the world so that we might live through him. Love consists in this: not that we loved God, but that he loved us and sent his Son to be the atoning sacrifice for our sins.' God is loving enough to want to bless us in any and every situation and He will never cease to be active for our good.

And the brilliant truth for those who are suffering is that God is utterly wise, utterly powerful and utterly loving all the time. There is never a time when He is lacking in wisdom, power or love.

And the consequence of that is that we are safe. We're not safe from sadness. We're not safe from the attrition of having to grind through days which are emotionally tough. We're not safe from feeling at the end of ourselves. But we are ultimately safe because our totally wise and powerful and loving God is always, always there for us, and there is nothing which can thwart His good purposes for us.

Knowing that helps. Being reminded of that helps. Doctrine helps.

That has shaped the way we have sought to help other people in their situations of suffering. We've often reminded people that suffering is, in the end, temporary. We've often prayed for people by appealing to God in His wisdom and power and love. We've sought to use the doctrines of God's word to bring encouragement to people in their situations of suffering.

You could do that too, couldn't you? If you're coming alongside someone who's dying of cancer, you could think in advance of doctrines which will help. If you're visiting someone who's coming to terms with a child's disability, you could work out before you go which truths from God's word would be most helpful to them. You don't have to be novel or edgy; you just have to point them to the truths of God's word.

One note of caution: it's important to be careful which doctrines you use and when you use them. Here's one example.

God is just. That truth, that doctrine, has often been a comfort to God's people in their times of need, especially in times of persecution at the hands of others. One day, all the injustices of this world will be righted. If that were not the case, life would hardly be worth living. Who wants to live in a world where people can commit the most appalling crimes and get away with it for ever?

But the truth that God is just can be misused and misapplied. In the early days of our suffering, one or two people came up to us asking whether we'd done something wrong that we should be going through so much. Those people believed in

God's justice but they committed exactly the same error as Job's friends who tenaciously held to the view that Job was suffering because of some sin in his life. Doctrine undergirded their words, but it was doctrine misused and misapplied. You can imagine how helpful it was to us – not!

Another example of someone misusing and misapplying doctrine sticks in our minds more than anything else, though. It was all to do with the sovereignty of God. When Jennie was expecting our second child, Livvy, she had a conversation with an older lady which went as follows.

Older lady: 'So, you're expecting again. Well done! You used folic acid this time, didn't you?' (Folic acid reduces the risk of spina bifida and other neural tube defects in many pregnancies.)

Jennie: 'Well, actually, I took folic acid religiously every day for years before we were expecting Elly.'

Older lady: 'Oh! Her spina bifida was obviously meant to be then.'

At which point, Jennie walked away (which was preferable to head-butting her).

Again, you can imagine how helpful that wasn't. That lady had a distorted view of God's sovereignty. Her words implied this: if Jennie hadn't been taking folic acid, having a baby with spina bifida would have been our fault; given that she was it must have been God's will. It's a denial of the fact that, as Ephesians 1:11 puts it, He 'works out everything in agreement with the purpose of his will'. 'Everything' really does mean 'everything' there.

So please be careful that you are using the doctrines of God's word correctly.

There's something else we need to say about using doctrine. Please make sure that you're bringing the right truths to bear at the right time. Here's an example.

We've also often found that when people are facing terminal illness, they're not ready in the early days of coming to terms with it to hear about heaven. They know they're going there but they're not quite ready to accept that it's time for them to go. They're wrestling with thoughts such as 'What's going to happen to my children? How will my wife cope? How come I've failed so much as a Christian?' They're not quite disengaged enough from life here and now to be ready to hear about life there and then.

So point them to Christ instead. Point them to the cross. Point them to God's sovereignty. The time will come when they're ready to hear about heaven. But tailor your doctrine to their immediate needs.

Doctrine helps. So as you come alongside your suffering friend, don't shy away from doctrine. Think in advance of what doctrines might help them: whether that's truth about God's character, truth about Jesus' redemption, truth about the Spirit's presence, truth about the age to come, or whatever. Bring them something substantial from the word of God because that's going to help them in a significant way.

12

Friendship Helps

The fourth thing we've learned about helping the suffering is this: friendship helps.

The Bible is very clear about the importance of friendship. The Book of Proverbs, for example, waxes lyrical about the beauty of friendship. Here's just one example, Proverbs 18:24: 'One with many friends may be harmed, but there is a friend who stays closer than a brother.' Friendship like that described in the second half of the proverb is of incalculable worth. To know that you have a friend who will be there with you through thick and thin… To know that someone will stand by you whatever you're going through… To know that you are not alone… That is very precious indeed. That is the value of friendship.

The Bible is also very clear about the importance of Christian fellowship, of that sense of partnership in God's kingdom which all believers in the Lord Jesus Christ ought to have. We should have this sense of being allies together in the battle which is the

Christian life, in the battle which is life itself. That's why Romans 12:15 commands us: 'Rejoice with those who rejoice; weep with those who weep.' We're to stand by each other, and we're to stand by each other in the best times and in the worst.

Over the years, we have increasingly learned the value of friendship. Jennie has always appreciated close friends; James hasn't always prioritized friendship. But we have both learned that friendship helps in times of need – and in times of ease. A good friend can be as invigorating as a cold water plunge pool after a sauna. Not that we've tried that!

The issue here is obvious: life is busy. There's work and family and church and housework and the need to eat and the need to make some time to sleep. Life is already very full for many people. We can very easily start to feel as though we have very little time for friends. In fact, we can very easily become wary of investing in friendships in case they take too much of our time. We factor in friendship almost as another entry on our to-do lists.

That is not the way we're meant to live. God Himself is a God of relationship. The closest relationship in the universe is the relationship of love between the three persons of the Godhead. What is more, that love spills out into a desire to have a relationship with us. Whatever else being made in the image of God might mean, surely it implies that we are relational beings. We need friendship. We need fellowship. Friendship helps.

We'll talk about the value of friends being there in the long-term in the next chapter. For now, we just want to encourage you to develop friendships with others and to be a good friend to those who are suffering because friendship helps.

Over the years, we've found that friendship helps in three ways.

First, it helps with spiritual support. If you action the last three chapters, you'll be giving that, so we won't say more about it here.

Second, friendship helps with emotional support.

Some time after her mother died, Jennie spent an evening with a few friends. Afterwards, she offered a lift to someone and drove her home. They chatted as they went and Jennie started to open up about how she was feeling about her grief. In the end, they sat outside her house for an hour-and-a-half, even though it was late, with Jennie talking and her friend just listening.

That was astonishingly precious to Jennie. She wanted to talk about her mum, but often when she did she would start crying. Many other people didn't know what to do with that and the conversation had ended at that point. But here was someone who listened, who let Jennie talk, who let her cry and who let her unburden herself without embarrassment or awkwardness. That moment really mattered.

And you could do that, couldn't you? You could meet up with a suffering friend. And you could offer emotional support. You could do that in many different ways.

Sometimes the only thing those who are suffering need is a hug. It can be as simple as that! There have been countless times for us when a hug has spoken more than a thousand words.

Sometimes those who are suffering simply need to be listened to. There can be so many thoughts and feelings seething away inside that it feels as though you're going to burst. It can be hard to think in a linear way. It can be hard to make sense of everything that is going on. Just to be able to talk about it with someone who is going to listen is an amazing blessing. To be able to unburden yourself with someone who loves you enough not to interrupt and not to try to answer all your problems and not to butt in with their own similar experiences and not to make you feel bad for the strong things you might say... That is very precious indeed. And you could be that listening ear, couldn't you?

Sometimes those who are suffering just need their woes to be validated. All suffering feels dreadful. Some suffering is appalling. Sometimes all a suffering person needs to hear is something like, 'Goodness me! That must be really hard. I can't imagine how awful that must feel!' And that's what they need to hear because it sanctions their grief. It takes their suffering seriously. It helps them to start to make sense of what is really going on. You could stand by someone like that, couldn't you? We've seen the difference it can make in people's lives.

Sometimes those who are suffering need guidance about what to do. When people are in the thick of it, it can be really hard to think straight. So many emotions and thoughts ambush them that they wonder whether they'll ever be able to think in a logical way again. So sometimes it might be appropriate to help a suffering friend to work out what to do. You may feel out of your depth in doing that, but don't worry too much about that. You can always encourage your friend to seek help from a church leader or from a professional counsellor or from someone else – which may involve you organising contact and maybe even going along with your friend. But for those who are suffering there are times when it can be a great emotional support just to have a friend who will sit with them and help them to see the next steps they need to take. Friendship helps.

Third, friendship helps with practical support.

There have been a few times over the years when one of us from the family has suddenly been hospitalized in the middle of the night. When that happens, we have some friends from the church who we ring. Imagine a 4 a.m. conversation like this as the husband picks up the phone.

(Speaking groggily and somewhat confused) 'Hello!'

'Hello! It's James. We need to go to the hospital again. Are you able to come over to look after the other kids, please?'

(Speaking groggily and somewhat confused) 'What?'

'It's James. We need to go to the hospital again. Can you come over to look after the other kids, please?'

(Speaking groggily and somewhat confused) 'Sure!'

And then ten minutes later, his wife arrives to look after the kids.

Others have helped us in other practical ways. There have been friends who have regularly done our ironing for us; we recently came back from holiday to find that someone had done all our ironing for us, even the clothes that had been at the bottom of the ironing basket for more than a year! There have been scores of friends who have cooked meals for us or who have organized rotas of people to cook meals for us. There have been friends who have looked after our children to create some space for us to talk. There have been friends who have helped with our garden or with decorating our house. We've been served in many, many ways.

To have a friend who will do those sorts of things counts. These days, families tend to be scattered all around the country. Our nearest relatives are about two hours' drive away. So the practical support which friends can offer really helps. We've come across examples of individuals almost adopting suffering families and helping them in all kinds of needed practical ways – and that's brilliant.

And you could offer practical support, couldn't you? You could find ways of providing practical support which really helps those who are suffering.

But please make that support specific.

Dave Furman is a pastor who's written a book about loving those who are hurting called *Being There*. Here's something he writes about offering help to those who are suffering.

Knowing how hard it is for people to ask for help, we need to offer assistance in a way that is easy to accept. When you pledge general help to someone in need, it's not likely that he or she will take you up on the offer. Sometimes a general offer of help just makes us feel good about ourselves. When we pledge general help, we put the burden on the hurting; we expect *them* to come up with a way for us to help. That's a tough assignment to put on someone grieving or in pain. They may not even be thinking clearly, and now they have to come up with a way that they can be helped.[1]

We've found that to be true. Worse, we've also encountered numerous examples of people who have said, 'Let me know if there's anything I can do,' but who, when we've asked for specific help, have made us feel guilty for asking. Others have offered help but haven't followed through. As you can imagine, that made us feel worse than we did before.

Practical support really helps but in giving practical support use your imagination. Work out what is really going to help and then offer to do it – or just do it! That sort of practical support is just what those who are suffering really value. You could do that, couldn't you? Friendship helps.

Friendship helps. It helps spiritually, emotionally and practically. So don't shy away from investing in friendships. Don't shy away from being a good friend. Be that friend who sticks closer than a brother.

---

1 Dave Furman, *Being There* (Wheaton, IL: Crossway, 2016), p. 125.

13

Being There for the Long Haul Helps

The fifth thing we've learned about helping the suffering is this: having people who are there for the long haul helps.

We mentioned earlier about the attrition which goes along with caring for someone with a disability. Any situation of long-term suffering will have its own form of attrition. If you are in constant pain, you are likely to be worn down by it in the long run. If you are suffering in a marriage which is loveless, you will probably find an ever-increasing sense of weariness in it. If you are struggling with loneliness, you may well find that your desperation grows as the years go by. Chronic situations of suffering have a way of eroding our strength, even if we don't sense it happening.

What is more, times when one thing seems to go wrong after another can have the same effect. The Book of Job is so helpful here. Job suffered wave after wave of agonising suffering. He loses his wealth. He loses most of his family. He loses his health. He's reduced to sitting on a heap of ashes, scraping his pustulating skin with a shard of broken pottery. And how he feels it! Taste his pain in Job 3:23-6: 'Why is life given to a man whose path is hidden, whom God has hedged in? I sigh when food is put before me, and my groans pour out like water. For the thing I feared has overtaken me, and what I dreaded has happened to me. I cannot relax or be calm; I have no rest, for turmoil has come.' Job is in anguish. In the original Hebrew, his words at the end of that passage read with a terrible staccato effect: Job is being machine gunned with pain.

What has surprised us is the fact that the attrition of what we've been through over the years has often been harder to deal with than the crises. What we suffered nearly a decade ago was very bitter but we've been ground down more by the day-in-day-out reality of disability and by the chasm left in our lives by the loss of Bev and Sam. We are still being upheld by the Lord – His grace is sufficient for us – but in the less spectacular grind of chronic sorrow and hardship, keeping going just feels, somehow, more challenging.

Alongside the fact that long-term or repetitive suffering has this attritional effect is the fact that life for everybody else moves on. That's very natural and right, of course. But we've often heard comments like these. 'For the first six months after my husband died, everyone asked me how I was. But then it just stopped.' 'My friends were great in the initial crisis, but now they just don't know what to do so they avoid the subject. It makes us feel unloved.'

There has been some of that in our experience too. We've made a point of asking for help when things have mounted up for us. But people have often quickly forgotten the ongoing nature of our situation. In lots of cases, their own lives have simply thrown up enough for them to deal with.

As you read that, we wouldn't want you to think that we're irritated with people or that we think they've abandoned us. If we're realistic, we know that these days as a family we have less time for people than we used to have. We've lost friends simply because we haven't had the time to keep up with them. Acquaintances from the past may well think of us as bad friends because we haven't been there for them as much as we used to be. There may even be some truth in that in some instances. We realize that not everyone can be there for the long haul for everyone.

Nevertheless being there for the long haul helps. If you want to support a friend who is suffering, keep on being there. You won't be able to do that for too many people all at the same time, of course. But be steadfast and be faithful. Keep involved for as long as you can because even one friend who does that can make an immense difference to someone who is suffering.

What might that look like? Well, use your imagination! Perhaps you could organize a monthly coffee date. Perhaps you could play tennis once a week. Perhaps you could ask your friend every so often how she is really doing. Perhaps you could do some ironing every few weeks. Perhaps you could babysit to create some downtime. Perhaps you could act as an honorary uncle or grandmother and just do things which support your friend and his wider family. Perhaps you could commit to praying every day. And there are many other things you could do too.

When other help has dried up, it's great just to have one or two people who are still there. Very deep bonds of friendship can be formed then so, please, think about who you could be a blessing to for the long haul.

There's one other thing we should talk about here. Married people have the blessing of being able to turn to each other at times of difficulty (unless, of course, the problem is an issue between them). And that can lead other people to imagine that they are receiving all the support they need from each other.

In actual fact, that may not be the case. It should be, of course. After the Lord, the first port of call a husband should turn to ought to be his wife and, after the Lord, the first port of call a wife should turn to ought to be her husband. But sometimes suffering husbands and wives can be at a loss to know how best to support one another. What is more, no married couple is an island. In our good times and in our bad times, we all still need the support of a wider community. Married couples should not be insular; every wife needs good friends and every husband needs good friends too.

We've carried out marriage preparation with many couples over the years. One of the things which has struck us most is that, usually, the husband-to-be and the wife-to-be have quite different personalities from one another. That can be a great strength in a marriage: the couple's combined personalities can cope with a greater range of situations than would have been the case if they had just been identical. But it can also be a recipe for tension between them.

As a couple we have different personalities. Jennie is emotionally expressive: we've lost count of how many times she's been in tears while we've been writing this book together. James is much less emotionally expressive, something which has become all the more acute as attrition has taken hold in his life. Jennie is quick at understanding and working out the implications of data (such as information we might be given at a hospital appointment). James needs a day or two to process things. Jennie finds it very hard to switch off her mind from thinking over difficult situations. James can lay things aside much more easily. Jennie tends to be more optimistic than James.

As a consequence of that, there have been times when we haven't always seen situations in the same way. We recall one time when Jennie was very upset after a hospital appointment. She was expressing her emotions freely. But James wasn't upset at all; he was still processing things and was yet fully to comprehend the implications of what we'd just been told. At that point we were at such different places that it became hard for us to support each other in the way we normally would.

Thankfully, we've been able to resolve issues like that quickly but some couples find that much harder to do. They can approach their situations of difficulty so differently that each hardly feels supported by the other at all. It's well known that crises can lead to the breakdown of marriages; each spouse's approach to the situation can be a part of the problem.

So if you're a woman supporting a married woman in a time of suffering, please don't quit just because you assume she's being well looked after by her husband. She may well be, but there may also be things which you can sympathize with her about, which her husband will just not relate to. Keep on encouraging her to share with her husband, of course; do all you can to protect and to support their marriage. But also be there for her for the long haul.

And if you're a man supporting a married man in a time of suffering, please don't quit just because you assume he's being well looked after by his wife. He may well be, but there may also be things which you can sympathize with him about, which his wife will just not relate to. Keep on encouraging him to share with his wife, of course; do all you can to protect and to support their marriage. But also be there for him for the long haul.

In speaking about married people here, we do not, of course, want to minimize the difficulties which single people have when they enter into a time of suffering. When single people suffer, it can throw up a unique problem for them: it may not be immediately obvious who they should turn to for support. That can be very isolating and painful. Apart from the Lord Himself, there is nobody more crucial then than long-standing friends.

What is more, where people are single because of separation or divorce or bereavement, it can be even harder. Where once there was someone on hand to speak to, now that person is no longer there. The heartache – and maybe even bitterness – which that can cause is often very difficult to deal with indeed. Long-standing friends can be absolutely vital then.

Proverbs 17:17 says, 'A friend loves at all times, and a brother is born for a difficult time.' Is there someone who you could love as a friend at all times? Is there someone you could be there for as weeks stretch into months and as months stretch into years? If so, be there! Because being there for the long haul helps.

14

Providence Helps

The sixth thing we've learned about helping the suffering is this: being reminded of the providence of God helps.

2 Corinthians 1:3-4 is a very significant passage in understanding the providence of God in suffering. The apostle Paul writes, 'Blessed be the God and Father of our Lord Jesus Christ, the Father of mercies and the God of all comfort. He comforts us in all our affliction, so that we may be able to comfort those who are in any kind of affliction, through the comfort we ourselves receive from God.' There are immense truths there for those who are going through it.

First, Paul tells us something about God. As he has suffered, Paul has come to know Him as 'the Father of mercies'. God the Father's heart goes out to us in our sufferings. There's sympathy for us in our troubles and difficulties and griefs. He cares.

What is more, God is also 'the God of all comfort'. He is the God who has a limitless capacity to comfort. He is the

God whose very nature is to comfort. He puts His unseen arm around our shoulders and relieves some of the pressure of our afflictions. That does not mean that He will always choose to take it away, but it does mean that He is able to refresh us, even as we suffer.

Of course, if we're to come to know God as 'the Father of mercies and the God of all comfort', then we need to suffer, don't we? We can know Him that way in theory in the good times, but we can only know Him that way by experiencing suffering. Suffering can be truly harrowing, but it might also be indispensable for drawing us deeper into a knowledge of God.

There's a second thing which Paul says about suffering in that passage, though. He says that when we've received comfort from God in our affliction, we are then able to use that comfort to comfort others. We're able to call upon our experience, our first-hand knowledge of God's comfort to support and to encourage others in their hard times.

When we first received Elly's diagnosis of spina bifida, someone we know who was suffering from chronic illness emailed us. This is what she said.

> There's very little that we can say that will mean anything, except that we will continue to pray for you both and for your little girl. You've been through a lot in the past few years and in the world's view it seems very unfair, but we know that in God's eyes you and your little girl are precious. He has each of your names engraved on the palms of His hands and knows all your thoughts and actions intimately.

We have no doubt that you will face testing times in the days, weeks, months and years ahead and that you will suffer. Never doubt that God is enough, that He can sustain you through it all, and that He will bring joy amidst great sadness. One thing that has been brought home to us over the past few years is that God is always enough – we are never too far from Him to find Him again and are never tested beyond what He is able to sustain us through. We're glad that in the midst of such hurt you are able to trust God and experience the peace He gives in your hearts.

That meant a lot to us. It's a great example of someone who has known God's comfort in affliction comforting us in our afflictions.

To sum it up: Paul is teaching us that God's providence is at work when we suffer. He uses our sufferings so that we can know Him better. He uses our sufferings to equip us to minister to others. He has His purposes in our hard times.

Having a consciousness of the providence of God has helped us in our sufferings. We can see how we have grown in our experience of Him as we've gone through each painful ordeal. We can see how we have received from Him, through the comfort He has given us, a depth of understanding of other people's situations. We can see how we have been given evangelistic opportunities which would never have come our way if we had not been through what we've been through. Looking back, we can see how God's providence has worked things out according to His perfect will – not that we could always see that at the time.

In many ways, our sufferings have refined our joint ministry. It's certainly narrower now: because of Elly's ongoing needs, we have less time available than we used to. But it's certainly deeper and we've been trained by God to support others in ways we couldn't before.

Being reminded of the providence of God helps. And you could point your friends to the predestining, fatherly purposes of God in their suffering, couldn't you? You can assure them that it's not for nothing. You can encourage them with the fact that there is nothing in this life which our Father in heaven will not overrule for the good of His people and for the promotion of His glory.

Now, there's a right and a wrong time to do all this. If your friend is in the throes of the deepest misery, it may not strike a chord with her that the Lord has purposes in her pain. At that point, maybe the best thing you can do is give her a hug, read a Bible verse to her, and pray with her. But at the right time, you can remind her of the providence of God. Having that wider perspective on suffering just helps.

Say you're with a friend who has been let down by someone close to her. There's been betrayal. And in the aftermath of it all, your friend is very, very low. She feels angry, yes. But alongside that she's started to think that there must be something wrong with her. She feels detested and despised and loathsome. She regularly breaks down at the memory of what has happened to her.

How can you help her? Well, just be there for her. Then at the right time, perhaps you can help her to start to make sense of her suffering. You can show her how it's increased her experiential knowledge of the Lord (though you might not use the word 'experiential' with her!); after all, Jesus knows what betrayal feels like from the inside. You can show her how it's equipped her to minister to others who have known the same sort of anguish. You can show her that it may even give her opportunities for the gospel as she models grace in upsetting times. Pick your time carefully but help her to see God's hand in her suffering. Knowing God's providence just helps.

There's something else to say here if you yourself are the one who has suffered. Do you see how God can use what you've been through to further His plans for the world? How could you use what you've learned about Him through the pain of divorce? How could you use what you've learned about Him through the misery of unfair remarks being made about your family? How could you use what you've learned about Him through the subtle opposition of your colleague at work which gnaws away at you? How could you use what you've learned about Him through the grinding apprehension of living with chronic illness? If you've suffered, please see God's providence in it and use what He's taught you for the blessing and the comfort of others. We'll be forever grateful to people who had struggled with infertility before us, for example, for sharing their experiences and their wisdom with us. They comforted us with the comfort they had received from Christ. They pointed us to the providence of God.

Being reminded of God's providence helps. So devote what you've suffered into the Lord's hands and use it for Him. Then seek to remind others of God's unseen but good purposes behind everything they're enduring.

15

Jesus Helps

The seventh thing we've learned about helping the suffering is this: Jesus helps. Naturally, this is the most important lesson of all.

It's an old joke that, whatever question you ask your Sunday School class, the answer is always 'Jesus'. In fact, Jesus is the ultimate answer to everything we face in life so if you truly want to help someone who is suffering, the very best thing you can do for them is to point them to the Lord Jesus Christ. Jesus helps.

Just think about His compassion, for example, as it's revealed in the Bible.

Think of Luke 7:13. Jesus and His disciples enter a town called Nain. As He approaches, He encounters a funeral procession. He takes in the scene and He can see who is at the centre of all that grief. It's a woman. She's already lost her husband and now she's lost her son. She's the picture of desolation.

Then we read this. 'When the Lord saw her, he had compassion on her and said, "Don't weep."' Jesus has compassion on her. His heart goes out to her. He's moved deep within: the Greek word used here speaks of Jesus feeling sympathy in His gut for this lady. He pities her deeply and in all her sorrow He goes up to her and He speaks. 'Don't cry,' He says. And then, as you'll know if you're aware of the passage, He raises her son back to life.

It's Jesus' compassion which shines out. It's a compassion which He feels, a compassion which is active, a compassion which reaches out to the woman in her need.

And this is just one example of the compassion of the Lord Jesus Christ.

Matthew 14 tells us about a time when Jesus goes off with the disciples for a bit of time-out but finds a great mass of people waiting for Him. Matthew 14:14 says, 'When he went ashore, he saw a large crowd, had compassion on them, and healed their sick.' We're not sure we would have been so compassionate if our plans for a bit of rest and relaxation had suddenly been ruined like that! But Jesus has compassion.

There's more in Mark 1:40-41, where a man with leprosy, and thus an outcast, comes and asks Him for help. 'Then a man with leprosy came to him and, on his knees, begged him: "If you are willing, you can make me clean." Moved with compassion, Jesus reached out his hand and touched him. "I am willing," he told him. "Be made clean."' Imagine the impact of that! Not just the healing but the compassion going along with it, the fact that

Jesus actually reached out His hand and touched him! How that man must have been comforted in the depths of his being.

There's a very famous example in Matthew 9:36. Jesus sees crowds of people who do not know the way to be saved. 'When he saw the crowds, he felt compassion for them, because they were distressed and dejected, like sheep without a shepherd.' Jesus appreciates the true need of the people. They're lost. They're dejected. They're guideless. They're harassed and helpless. And He feels the deepest compassion for them.

That is the compassion of Jesus. Compassion towards those who have suffered loss. Compassion towards those in need. Compassion towards the outcast. Compassion towards the lost. Jesus is the most compassionate person who has ever lived. Jesus Christ. God the Son made man. The most powerful, most important, most significant, most authoritative person who has ever lived. And yet moved with compassion, His heart going out to people, feeling the deepest sympathy towards needy people.

We haven't even mentioned the cross yet. What could ever show the compassion of Jesus more intensely than the cross? There He gave Himself to the uttermost, taking the pain due to us for our sin, taking the very wrath of God Himself which we should have suffered eternally because of our guilt. That is compassion written in the largest letters upon the canvas of the universe.

Jesus, of course, is risen. He's ascended into the heavenly realms and the good news for us today is that Jesus is just as compassionate now as He ever was when He walked this earth. Hebrews 4:15 talks about how He sympathizes with us. 'For we do not have a high priest who is unable to sympathize with our weaknesses, but one who has been tempted in every way as we are, yet without sin.' Jesus sympathizes with us. He's no detached observer. He's been there. He knows what it's like. He's known greater depths of suffering than we can ever know. And He sympathizes with us. He suffers with us. He feels with us. He has compassion towards us.

What could be more amazing than that?

There have been times in our sufferings when Jesus has been unbelievably precious to us. We've experienced His compassion. We've felt His kindness. We've tasted His mercy. We've set Him before us and we've known Him propping us up. He's been there to bind up our wounds. He's been close to us when we've been brokenhearted. What a Saviour we have!

The very best thing you can do for your suffering friends is to point them to Jesus. Remind them of Him. Remind them of His compassion. Remind them of those Bible verses about His care for them. Remind them of His other attributes too: His power and faithfulness and patience and kindness and wisdom. Remind them of the cross. Point them to Jesus because He is always the answer.

When Bev was nearing the end of her life, she read some articles by Mark Ashton. He was a vicar from Cambridge who wrote about facing death when he was diagnosed with terminal cancer. He died just under a year before her. His words have since been published in a little book called *On My Way to Heaven*.

Here are two little sections from what Mark Ashton writes.

Every one of us will face up to God to answer for our lives, and every one of us will hang our heads in shame as we realise that we have to be condemned for the way we have lived in God's world as if it were our own world. But, even as my condemnation is announced, my Redeemer will rise at last (Job 19:25), and Jesus will present incontrovertible evidence that my sentence has been fully carried out when he died in my place on the cross. It is my relationship with him that can take me through death and which is the only hope we have of eternal life. He alone is the destroyer of death....

It is in terms of relating to him that I must understand my death. Jesus will be the same – indeed, he will be more real and more true than he ever has been before. It will be his voice that will call me into his presence (1 Thess. 4:16). He will take me to be with him (John 14:3), so that I may be with him forever (1 Thess. 4:17). He is the first and the last (Rev. 1:17-18), the beginning and the end (Rev. 21:6). It has been said that, for the believer, the end of the world is more of a person than it is an event. That is certainly true of the end of my life. My death may be the event with which my physical life on earth ends, but it will also be the moment at which my relationship with Jesus becomes complete. That relationship is the only thing that has made sense of my physical life, and at my death it will be everything.[1]

---

1   Mark Ashton, *On My Way to Heaven* (Lancashire, England: 10 Publishing, 2010), pp. 27-30.

As Bev faced her own death, those words just helped her. They gave her immense encouragement deep down. They pointed her to the Lord Jesus Christ. And the thought of being with Him in heaven became sweeter and sweeter as her day approached. She never knew Mark Ashton but he pointed her to Christ and by doing so, he helped to carry her towards the day when she would meet Him for herself.

Don't you want to be involved in doing something like that? When people you know suffer, talk to them about Jesus. There's nothing in the entire world which is more nourishing than feeding people with the bread of life.

It's possible that you're helping someone who is not a Christian and who is going through a period of intense suffering. If that is the case, you can follow some of the advice from Chapters 1 to 6 with them. But their greatest need is Jesus. So as you come alongside them, please above all else seek opportunities to point them to Him. Paint a glorious picture of Him as your Saviour, your helper, your friend, your brother, your Lord. And recommend Him to them in what you say and what you do. Who knows whether, actually, your friend's suffering may become the opening for the greatest blessing of their lives as they come to know and trust Him too?

A few years ago, we knew a man who had suffered greatly in his younger years. He'd fled from his home country which was a dangerous place to live. He'd ended up in a European country as an illegal immigrant, and he'd been imprisoned for three months.

Those three months were the most miserable for his life. The prisoners were held 100 to a room with only two toilets and one cold shower between them. They slept on the concrete floor. Years later, he wrote, 'Despite the physical sufferings, which bring tears to my eyes even now, the hardest part was being totally isolated and cut off from family and friends.' He missed everyone he loved desperately.

Then a Christian visited him. It was a Christian who spoke his language. He hugged him and brought him food and clothes. When he was allowed to leave prison, he picked him up and took him to his home. He pointed him to Jesus.

Eventually, our friend was converted. He sought out other Christians who pointed him to Christ, and before too long he came to know and to love Jesus as His own Lord and Saviour. It all started with a Christian supporting him in his suffering and introducing him to Jesus. There's nothing that thrills the soul more than when that happens!

You could be part of that, couldn't you? Whoever you're coming alongside, Jesus helps. The Bible helps. Prayer helps. Doctrine helps. Friendship helps. Being there for the long haul helps. Providence helps. But nothing helps like Jesus. So as you help and support your suffering friends, point them to Him. And see what He will do!

Acknowledgements

We're grateful to so many people for their help in writing this book. We are most grateful to God for our parents and siblings: in lots of ways our story is their story too – parts of it more theirs than ours. They've been a massive support to us, as well as shaping our characters as they brought us up, and we love them dearly.

We would like to thank Carey Baptist Church in Reading for giving James a sabbatical; without this we would never have carved out the time to put fingers to keyboards. We're especially grateful to our sabbatical support team, John and Sharon Seymour and Alistair and Sue Murdoch, for their encouragement along the way: they also made numerous suggestions which improved the book immensely.

We're thankful for the staff at Christian Focus for all the help they've given as we've walked the road towards publishing for the first (and maybe last!) time.

Above all else, of course, we're thankful to the Lord who has carried us day by day. We're so grateful to Him for each other, for our children, for our wider families, and for all the friends He's connected us with. As the years have gone by, we've found that the one who loves us so much that He gave His Son for us is more than enough. We can face whatever may come with His help.